DISCARD

DUE DATE

BEAUTIFUL
Wedding Crafts

BEAUTIFUL

Wedding Crafts

GIFTS, DECORATIONS & KEEPSAKES TO MAKE & CHERISH

Heidi Tyline King & Nancy Worrell

LARK BOOKS

Asheville, North Carolina

Editor: Laura Dover Doran

Art Direction: Celia Naranjo

Photography: Evan Bracken

Illustrations: Heidi Tyline King

Editorial Assistant: Heather Smith

Production Assistant: Hannes Charen

Flower photography on pages 5, 107, and 127: Richard Babb

Library of Congress Cataloging-in-Publication Data
King, Heidi.
    Beautiful wedding crafts : gifts, decorations, and keepsakes to
make and cherish / Heidi Tyline King & Nancy Worrell. —1sted.
        p.   cm.
    ISBN 1-57990-084-4 (hc.)
    1. Handicraft. 2. Wedding decorations. 3. Weddings—Equipment and supplies.
    4. Gifts. I. Worrell, Nancy. II. Title.
    TT149.K557   1999

745.549'1—DC21   98-36128
                                                                  CIP

10 9 8 7 6 5 4 3 2

Published by Lark Books
50 College St.
Asheville, NC 28801, US

© 1998, Heidi Tyline King and Nancy Worrell

For information about distribution in the U.S., Canada, the U.K., Europe, and Asia, call Lark Books at 828-253-0467.

Distributed in Australia by Capricorn Link (Australia) Pty Ltd., P.O. Box 6651, Baulkham Hills Business Centre, NSW 2153, Australia

Distributed in New Zealand by Southern Publishers Group, 22 Burleigh St., Grafton, Auckland, NZ

Printed in Hong Kong by Oceanic Graphic Printing Productions Ltd.

Contents

Introduction

"The love we give away is the only love we keep."

—Elbert Hubbard

Every bride and groom deserve a perfect wedding day. Yet as weddings become more expensive with each passing year, sometimes it seems that the fairy tale is out of reach. As mother and daughter, we are very aware of the high cost of planning and celebrating a wedding to remember. Our first encounter with wedding sticker-shock came when we were planning Heidi's wedding. Not only did the cost of a wedding gown seem equivalent to a down payment on a car, but the gifts, decorations, and last-minute purchases quickly added up to more than we had wanted to spend. What's more, we were disappointed with the slim selection of wedding accessories. When we finally found something we liked, the quality wasn't as high as the price.

This book is our endeavor to provide beautiful options for newlyweds, the wedding party, family, and friends. We have chosen projects that will make the wedding day and every day following as fantastic and original as possible—without breaking your budget. You will find beautiful and unusual projects for celebrating the wedding of a lifetime and adding a personal touch to that first home together. Use the simple instructions and diagrams to craft sentimental presents and one-of-a-kind gifts, or to create heirlooms-to-be that reflect your personal touch. These handcrafted gifts can be given as tokens of appreciation by the bride to her wedding party or by family and friends to that special couple. Page after page offers a wide array of crafts, a multitude of ideas, and helpful hints that will help you capture the essence of a fairy-tale wedding.

Whether you are the bride, a member of the wedding party, or a wedding guest, you are sure to find an heirloom to craft or a unique gift to mark the celebration. Create these wonderful projects with love and share them in happiness.

A successful craft project begins with knowing the basics. Most of the projects in this book, though they vary widely in technique, require only basic crafting skills. Although this is also true of the sewing projects, we've provided basic sewing information in this section for your reference.

Embroidery Tips

• Before beginning work, practice stitching on a scrap piece of fabric.

• Avoid using knots. Instead, use one long strand of embroidery thread. Fold the thread in half and thread the needle with both cut ends. Beginning on the wrong side of the fabric, push the needle through the fabric to the right side, leaving the looped end of the thread on the wrong side. Bring the needle and thread back through the fabric and through the folded loop of thread. This will secure your thread without using a knot. You can also run thread ends under the stitches you have already made.

• Press all embroidery work on a well-padded ironing board so as not to flatten stitches.

Basic Embroidery Stitches

Backstitch. Make a short stitch. Insert the needle at the beginning of this stitch and bring it out a stitch ahead. Repeat across. The result should resemble machine-stitching and be neat and regular.

Blanket Stitch. Come up through the fabric about ¼ inch (.5 cm) in from the edge. Holding the thread with your thumb, go down and back up through the fabric at the edge, bringing the needle under the thread and pulling the stitch into place. Continue by pulling thread back up through the fabric about ¼ inch (.5 cm) in from the edge and ¼ inch (.5 cm) away from the first stitch.

Chain Stitch. Come up through the fabric and shape the thread into a loop. Go back down and up again through the fabric as shown, bringing the needle over the thread. Pull until the loop is the desired size. To end, take the needle down over the end of the last loop.

Cross Stitch. Make parallel straight stitches as shown, then reverse with parallel straight stitches to create crosses.

Fern Stitch. Pull the needle up through the fabric at the top end of one stitch. Push the needle down through the bottom end of the stitch, then pull it back up through the top of a second stitch. Repeat until all stitches are complete. Each fern stitch is generally the same length.

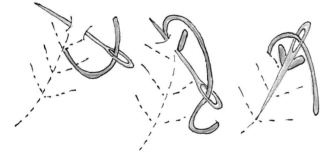

French Knot. Bring the tip of the needle up to the right side of the fabric. Wrap the thread around the needle two or three times or more, depending on the size of the knot desired. Insert the needle close to where it came out. While adjusting the tension with your free hand, pull the needle to the wrong side of the fabric to form a knot.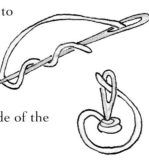

Lazy Daisy Stitch. Bring the needle up through the fabric. Insert the needle near where the thread came out then bring the needle up through the fabric again, keeping the thread under the needle. Draw up. This makes a loop which should lie flat. Insert the needle where the thread came out and take another stitch in same manner. Keep stitches the same length. Stitches are worked around a center point to form daisy.

Running Stitch. This is the simplest of all stitches. It is created by pulling the needle up through the fabric and pushing it down through the fabric, spacing the entry point and departure point to the desired length. The running stitch is a basic stitch in both sewing and embroidery. Stitches may be long or short as needed.

Satin Stitch. Pull the needle up through the fabric at one side of the design. Push the needle down through the fabric at the other side of the design. Pull the needle up on the first side as close as possible to the first stitch. Push the needle down on the opposite side as close as possible to the first stitch. Continue until the entire design is covered with thread.

General Stitches
and Techniques

Fringing. To self fringe, draw a thread out where you want the fringe to end. Machine-stitch along this line. Pull threads out to this stitching line. To knot fringe, count off two or more strands and tie an over-hand knot, pulling knot to edge of fabric. See page 98 for an example.

Lark's Head Knot. Fold ribbon or thread in half. Thread folded loop through hole or over bow. Bring ends of ribbon or thread up and through folded loop. Pull up to form knot.

Mock Flat-Fell Seam or Lapped Seam. This is done on the right side of the garment. Turn under one seam allowance and lap over the other. Stitch along folded edge.

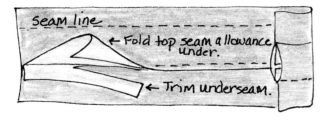

Slip Stitch or Blind Stitch. Pick up a thread or two of the fabric; then run needle inside folded edge about ¼ inch (.5 cm) and again pick up a thread or two. This stitch is often used for hemming skirts and dresses.

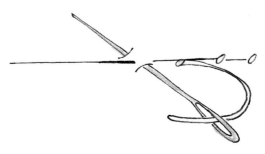

Needles

• Beading needles are slim wire needles, sometimes as long as 3 inches (7.5 cm), which are made especially for beadwork. They have a slender, elongated eye.
• Chenille needles are short, large-eyed needles with sharp points. They are ideal for stitching coarse materials with a heavy thread.
• Embroidery needles have long eyes for easy threading with one or more strands of floss.
• Sharp, multipurpose household sewing needles are short with round eyes.

Transferring Patterns

Helpful tools you may want to have on hand for transferring patterns are tracing paper, carbon paper, dressmaker's carbon paper, a dressmaker's pen and chalk pencil, a water-soluble marker, a black felt-tipped permanent marker, a pencil, white and colored pencils, a ruler, scissors, and a craft knife. The method you use to transfer the pattern will depend on the type of material to which the pattern will be transferred.

To transfer simple patterns to most fabrics, lay tracing paper on the printed pattern and trace. Cut out the traced pattern on the outline. Pin pattern to the fabric and trace around pattern.

To transfer patterns to light-colored, light-weight fabrics or paper, first trace or photo-copy the pattern. Retrace the outline with a black marker. Tape the tracing to a window pane or light box, then tape the material over the tracing. Using a water-soluble marker, trace the pattern onto the material.

To transfer patterns to solid or opaque mater-ial, such as dark fabric or card-stock paper, first trace the pattern. Stack the material (right side up), the carbon paper (carbon side down), and the tracing of the pattern (right side up). With a dull pencil, trace over the pattern to transfer the carbon outline to the material.

To transfer embroidery patterns, trace the design onto tracing paper, then poke holes along the outline with a pushpin. Mark over the lines with a dressmaker's chalk pencil so that the chalk is imprinted on the fabric.

Always transfer placement and guide markings as well as the outline to the traced pattern and material.

Bias Strips

Fabric that has been cut on the bias has extra stretchability. To cut a bias strip, fold fabric at a 45° angle so the cross-grain threads run parallel to the selvage or the lengthwise grain. Press and fold along the diagonal line to form a true bias. Open the fabric flat and cut on the fold. Measure and cut strips in the desired width.

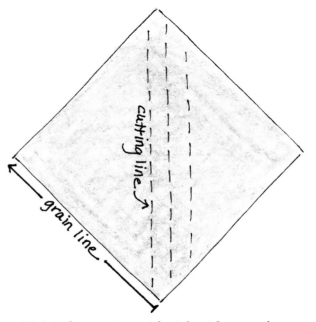

To join bias strips, with right sides together, overlap the ends of two strips at a 45° angle. Machine-stitch in place and trim ends.

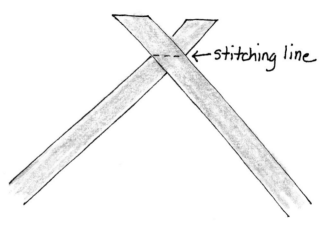

Once He Proposes

There will never be another time in your life quite like the time when you are engaged. Like a butterfly's cocoon, engagement is a magically strange interim between an old life and a new one. A multitude of important decisions must be made—choices that will be captured in wedding photographs to become cherished memories for years to come.

In this chapter, you'll find craft ideas to help you plan for that special day. From the beginning of your engagement, use the trio of attractive fabric-covered organizers to coordinate wedding plans. Look over the invitation designs for unique ideas you can pass along to friends hosting prenuptial parties, or use the ideas yourself to design one-of-a-kind thank-you notes.

You'll also find pretty gifts to make for bridesmaids, groomsmen, and hostesses. And for those stressful moments and prewedding jitters, relax and calm yourself by stealing an afternoon nap against the soothing lavender fragrance of a sweet dreams pillow.

"*What greater thing is there for two human souls*
than to feel that they are joined for life."

— George Eliot

Keepsake Wedding Album

We've designed a wedding album that's as functional as it is beautiful. Made with a purchased three-ring binder, this album is roomy enough for your wedding photographs, snapshots from your parties and showers, and all the keepsakes you can fit into purchased plastic pockets. It's not only a simple afternoon project, but it can also be made for a fraction of the cost of a store-bought album.

- 1 yard moiré or floral taffeta
- 1 yard (.9 m) satin ribbon in complementary color, 1½ inches (4 cm) wide
- ½ yard (.5 m) wired ribbon, 1½ inches (4 cm) wide, cut in half
- ½ yard (.5 m) fusible web
- 1-inch-thick (2.5-cm) three-ring binder
- Iron
- Pressing cloth
- Hot-glue gun and glue sticks (optional)
- Floral wire

Instructions

1. Press fabric and ribbons on low heat. Working on a flat surface, lay fusible web on wrong side of fabric and iron in place. Take care not to scorch fabric. Remove paper backing.

2. Open binder and position face down. Center fabric on top of binder, leaving at least a 3-inch (7.5-cm) overhang on each side. Using a damp pressing cloth, iron fabric to binder.

3. Trim edges of fabric to 2 inches (5 cm) and turn to inside of binder, cutting to fit as needed. Iron in place. If desired, use hot glue to secure edges.

4. To make the lining, cut two pieces of fabric 1 inch (2.5 cm) larger than each side of the binder. Turn all edges under 1½ inches (4 cm) and press. Lay fusible web on wrong side of fabric and iron in place. Remove paper backing.

5. Position lining pieces on inside of album and iron in place, fitting around three-ring spine and adjusting as needed to ensure all raw edges are covered.

6. Tie the satin ribbon into a bow. Trim tails of ribbons on bow diagonally to prevent raveling.

7. To make roses, cut ½ yard (.5 m) of wire ribbon in half. Remove wire from one edge of one piece of ribbon. To form rose center, tightly roll 1½ inches (4 cm) of the unwired end of the ribbon; stitch to secure. Loosely wrap the remaining ribbon around the rose center and stitch to secure. Fold the raw edge at the end of the ribbon to the bottom and stitch in place. Repeat step 7 to make another rose.

8. Tightly wire bottoms of roses together with floral wire to form a miniature bouquet. Attach roses to back of bow with floral wire. Center roses and bow on front of album and hot-glue securely in place.

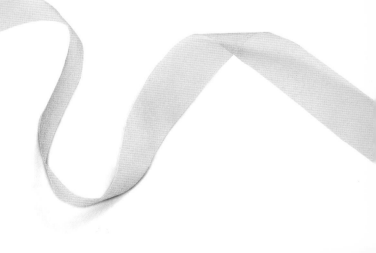

If you have good intentions of putting together a detailed wedding album but can't seem to find the time to do it, consider crafting a memory box instead. Dog-eared love letters, photographs with tattered edges, even playbills and ticket stubs from your honeymoon can be safely tucked away inside this beautiful box. A medium-weight fabric works best; if you choose a dark-colored box, be sure to use dark fabric.

- 1½ yards (1.4 m) taffeta fabric for box and lining
- 1½ yards (1.4 m) fusible web
- Sturdy box with lid. (Boot boxes, business-size envelope boxes, or hatboxes work well.)
- 2 yards (1.8 m) grosgrain ribbon in complementary color, 2 inches wide (5 cm) for edge of box top
- 2 yards (1.8 m) grosgrain ribbon in complementary color, 1 inch wide (2.5 cm) for edge of box top
- 1 yard (1.8 cm) grosgrain ribbon in complementary color, 2 inches wide (5 cm) for bow
- Iron
- Pressing cloth
- Hot-glue gun and glue sticks

Instructions

1. Press fabric and ribbon on low heat. Working on a flat surface, lay fusible web on wrong side of fabric and iron in place. Take care not to scorch fabric. Remove paper backing.

2. Center box on wrong side of fabric, leaving at least a 3-inch (7.5-cm) overhang on each side.

3. Using a damp pressing cloth, iron fabric to bottom of box and to short sides. Fold fabric over box corners to long sides and cut ½ inch (1.5 cm) from the corner edges. Trim excess fabric and press fabric in place.

4. Press fabric to long sides of box, trimming excess fabric and turning edges under so that all corners are covered and no raw fabric edges are showing.

5. Trim raw edges of fabric to 2 inches (5 cm) and turn to the inside of box. Iron in place. If desired, use hot glue to secure edges.

What Most Wedding Guides Don't Mention

• Include detailed maps for out-of-town guests in your wedding invitations. Make sure there is a telephone number for those who get lost.

• If you will be driving to your honeymoon destination, make sure that you have your car serviced at least two weeks before your trip.

• If possible, pack your going-away bag several days before your wedding to prevent leaving necessities behind. Include pertinent identification, necessary prescriptions, important telephone numbers, something to do or read en-route, and—if there's room—a small sewing kit and a first-aid kit.

• While you're away, have a neighbor or friend keep an eye on your home. Request that paper and mail delivery be stopped, find a kennel or pet sitter for your pet, and make sure your plants get watered.

---

6. Repeat steps 1 through 5 to cover lid.

7. To make the lining, cut a piece of fabric equal to the perimeter of the box plus 1 inch (2.5 cm) (length of fabric) and the depth of the box plus 1 inch (2.5 cm) (width of fabric).

8. Apply fusible web to the wrong side of the lining and press. Remove paper backing.

9. Turn long edges and one short edge of fabric under ½ inch (1.5 cm) and press to finish off edges.

10. Position lining inside box so that edges overlap; press in place. Secure fabric with hot glue, if needed, in hard-to-reach areas.

11. Position 2-inch-wide (5-cm) ribbon (here, we've used ivory ribbon) around box top; hot-glue in place, turning ends under in the center of the box. Center 1-inch-wide (2.5-cm) ribbon (white) over 2-inch-wide (5-cm) ribbon; hot-glue in place, again turning ends under. Trim excess ribbon.

12. Cut remaining 2-inch-wide (5-cm) ribbon into a 10-inch (25.5-cm) length; fold ends together and secure with hot glue. Fold another piece of ribbon around the center to form a flat bow. Hot-glue ribbon to the top of the box over layered ribbons (where ends are turned under).

Handmade Stationery with Party Pizzazz

Say it in style with unique stationery handcrafted from homemade papers, scraps of lace, fabric, thread, small trinkets, and faux flowers. Each invitation can be tailored to fit any type of wedding event, from prenuptial parties to post-wedding thank-you notes. If you don't want to write a personal note on each card, simply print the message on a computer, photocopy on clear acetate, cut to size, and tuck inside the invitation.

Bridal Bouquet. Always a bridesmaid, never a bride…Here's a miniature bouquet for those friends who dream of having their own bouquet. Purchase a bundle of tiny white roses, stems intact, and a heavy paper card. Punch two holes ½ inch (1.5 cm) apart in the center of card. Position bouquet on card front, thread a piece of ribbon through holes, and tie ribbon into a bow.

Flower Power. The rough texture of a hand-made-paper card contrasts nicely with the smooth, curvy lines of a fabric flower. Trim the stem to about 3 inches (7.5 cm), then carefully poke stem through the top of the card. If needed, secure flower in place by taping the stem to the inside of the card.

Thanks for the Memories. What better way to thank friends and family after the wedding than to present them with their own miniature photo album? Purchase an art-quality length of heavy card stock (available at most art supply stores), then fold the paper accordion-style at least four times. Punch a hole in the center of the front and back of the card, ⅛ inch (.3 cm) from the edge. Cut snapshots to desired size and secure to card with purchased photo corners. Thread thin ribbon through holes and tie into a bow.

Hear the Bells. This quick and easy wedding bells card is made by tearing a square from purchased handmade paper, then embellishing it with silver scrapbook stickers. Thread a silver cord around the fold of the card and tie on the outside.

▲ *On a Roll.* Though it would be impractical to mail a scrolled card, it's a touching way to deliver a heartfelt message to a nearby friend or family member. Simply purchase a piece of handmade paper, score the edges with a ruler, then carefully tear away at the score line to deckle the edges. Write your message, then roll it up and seal with a bow.

Picture This. Go ahead, rub in that fabulous honeymoon trip to Tahiti. If you took a spectacular photo, share it with friends by using it on your thank-you notes. Glue a piece of colorful corrugated cardboard to the front of a note card. Trim photograph to fit on card front, then secure with purchased photo corners. ▼

Sentimental Stencils. Victorian-style motifs are perennial favorites for wedding stationery. To make this stenciled card, begin with a heavy-weight note card. Lightly spray card front with glitter paint. Position heart stencil in center of card front and spray again to stencil design with glitter paint. Punch two holes in top center of card front, insert sheer ribbon, and tie ribbon into a bow.

◀ *In Stitches.* Machine-stitching on paper is an unusual crafting technique that is a wonderful way to create custom cards. For this collage, gather bits of thread and handmade paper and place on the front of a note card. Position a sheer organdy heart on top of the thread and paper, then machine-stitch in place with gold metallic thread.

Wedding File

Keep track of fabric swatches, photographs of wedding dresses, cost estimates, honeymoon brochures, scribbled lists of things to do, and a bride-to-be's hectic schedule with this pretty organizer.

- 1 yard (.9 m) moiré wedding fabric
- 2 yards (1.8) grosgrain ribbon in a complementary color, 1½ or 2 inches wide (4 or 5 cm)
- 1 yard (.9 m) fusible web
- Standard-size accordion file
- Iron
- Hot-glue gun and glue sticks
- Stapler
- Fabric glue

1. Press fabric and ribbon on low heat. Working on a flat surface, lay fusible web on wrong side of fabric and iron in place. Take care not to scorch fabric. Remove paper backing.

2. For the outside of the file, cut a piece of fabric the width of the file plus 4 inches (10 cm) and the length of the file and flap plus 4 inches (10 cm).

3. Open flap of accordion file and lay flap face down. Center fabric over file, wrong side down, leaving at least a 2-inch (5-cm) overhang on each side. Iron fabric in place.

4. Trim fabric edges to 1 inch (2.5 cm) around accordion file, then turn edges to the inside of the flap and file. Iron in place. For hard-to-reach spots, secure fabric with hot glue, trimming fabric as needed.

5. Fold ribbon in half and position ribbon so that the fold is 1 inch (2.5 cm) from and parallel to the inside edge of the front flap; hot-glue fold to the inside of the flap. Secure ribbon with stapler.

6. Cut remaining fabric to fit inside of flap, adding ½ inch (1.5 cm) to all sides. Turn fabric edges under ¾ inch (2 cm) and press in place on flap. If needed, secure edges with hot glue.

7. To close, fold top ribbon to outside of the flap; glue in place with fabric glue over staples. When dry, wrap ribbon around file and tie into a bow.

An accordion file without a flap can also be used.

Doorknob Sachets

These sachets are easy to stitch from scraps of velvet and eyelet and are the perfect size for hanging on a doorknob or tucking away in luggage. If you are making them for the wedding couple, pin a "Do Not Disturb" sign to the front of the sachet.

- Fabric scraps
- Polyester fiberfill
- 1 teaspoon or more of lavender seeds or potpourri (for each sachet)
- Scraps of ribbon, trims, pearls, and rosettes (see instructions below)
- 24-inch (62-cm) piece of ribbon, cut in half

1. Transfer two heart patterns (see page 10) to the fabric and cut out.

2. With right sides together and raw edges aligned, stitch hearts together, leaving a 2-inch (5-cm) opening for turning. Press and clip seams and turn.

fold of fabric →

Enlarge 200%.

3. Stuff heart sachet with fiberfill, mixing lavender or potpourri in as you go. Hand-stitch opening closed.

4. To make the pink pearl heart, whipstitch a strand of pearls along the seam line of the heart, beginning and ending at the top center of the heart. Randomly hand-stitch pearls on the front of the heart.

5. To make the eyelet heart, hand-stitch cording along the seam line, beginning and ending at the top center of the heart. Position a heart doily or scrap of ribbon to front of heart, then tack in place. Tack a small rosette to the center top of the doily.

6. To make the bow and hanger, fold a 12-inch (30.5-cm) piece of ribbon in half and tack the ends to the top of each heart. Tie a bow with remaining ribbon and tack bow over the ends of the hanger.

What Most Wedding Guides Don't Mention

If you plan to change your last name, be prepared to fill out dozens of name-change forms—so the earlier you get started, the better. (You can usually call an organization's office to find out how to obtain the appropriate form.) Here's a checklist to get you started.

- Driver's license
- Car registration
- Passport
- Social security card
- Insurance policies and wills
- Post office
- Voter registration
- Checking and savings accounts
- Magazines and other subscriptions
- Employee and/or student ID cards
- Stock certificates
- Credit cards and/or student loans
- Library card

Sweet Dreams Pillows

In Victorian times, tiny pillows filled with lavender were tucked underneath one's head to revive the spirits and relieve headaches. What a luxurious way to end a stressful day! It won't take long to craft a pillow for yourself or a bride-to-be. Here, we've used doilies and scraps of ribbon, but you can use any materials you have on hand.

Lavender Doily Pillow *(left)*

Materials

- Two 8-inch-diameter (20.5-cm) ecru fabric circles
- Polyester fiberfill
- 1 teaspoon lavender seeds or potpourri
- Two 8-inch-diameter (20.5-cm) ecru crocheted doilies
- 1 yard (.9 m) ecru organza ribbon, 1¼ inch (3 cm) wide
- Sprigs of dried lavender
- 18 inches (45.5 cm) ivory satin ribbon, ⅛ inch (.3-cm) wide

Instructions

1. With right sides together and raw edges aligned, stitch a ½-inch (1.5-cm) seam around the edges of the ecru circles, leaving a 3-inch (7.5-cm) opening. Press and turn to the right side. Stuff with polyester fiberfill and lavender or potpourri. Slip-stitch opening closed.

2. Center one doily on each side of the cotton pillow. Tack edges of doilies to pillow between scallops.

3. Tie a bow with the organza ribbon. Position lavender on top of bow and tie together with thin ivory ribbon. Tack bouquet to top of pillow.

Heart Pillow *(above)*

Materials

- 2 (6½-inch or 16.5-cm) squares of 14-count ecru Aida cloth
- Red pearl cotton thread, size 8
- 5-inch (12.5-cm) square of cream-colored tulle
- Red quilt thread
- Gold metallic sewing thread
- 1 tablespoon dried red rose petals
- 3 yards (2.7 m) red embroidery ribbon
- Polyester fiberfill

- Potpourri
- 1 yard (.9 m) red and gold cording, ³⁄₁₆ inch wide (.48 cm)
- Chenille needle
- Embroidery hoop
- Sewing machine
- Dressmaker's marker

Instructions

1. To make pillow front, mark a 3-inch (7.5 cm) square in the center of one piece of cloth.

2. Using red pearl cotton thread and a chenille needle, outline center square by stitching a running stitch at two-thread intervals across fabric square. Repeat to complete all squares.

3. To make the heart, thread sewing machine with red quilt thread and bobbin with gold metallic sewing thread.

4. Place tulle in embroidery hoop. Using medium-length stitch, machine-stitch tulle at ½-inch (1.5-cm) intervals to create a checkerboard pattern. Remove tulle from embroidery hoop.

5. Position heart frame pattern on tulle so that checkerboard design is crosswise of heart. Using dressmaker's marker, transfer heart pattern to stitched tulle.

6. Place tulle in embroidery hoop again, positioning the heart frame design in the center.

7. Using the red thread and a small zigzag stitch, sew around inside and outside edge of heart frame. Continue filling heart frame with zigzag stitches. Remove tulle from embroidery hoop.

8. Trim away tulle along outside of heart frame.

9. Position trimmed heart frame diagonally on stitched pillow top. Pin or baste in place, leaving a 2-inch (5-cm) opening for inserting rose petals.

10. Insert rose petals and slip-stitch opening closed.

11. Using the silk ribbon and chenille needle, blanket-stitch around outside edge of heart to secure heart to pillow top.

12. Repeat blanket stitch around inside edge of heart frame.

13. To complete pillow, with right sides facing, stitch pillow squares together, leaving a 3-inch (7.5-cm) opening for turning. Clip corners and turn.

14. Stuff with fiberfill and potpourri; hand-stitch opening closed.

15. Using needle and coordinating thread, blindstitch cording around outside edge of pillow. If desired, make a loop for hanging pillow by looping cording at upper corner.

Antique Linen Pillow

Materials

- 9-inch-square (23-cm) cutwork handkerchief
- Metallic thread
- Small pearl beads (number will vary, depending on handkerchief)
- Two ¾-inch-diameter (2-cm) gold and pearl buttons
- Two 6½-inch (16.5-cm) squares of muslin
- Polyester fiberfill
- 1 teaspoon potpourri of your choice
- 12-inch (30.5-cm) length of ¼-inch (.5-cm) gold and white ribbon

Instructions

1. Lay handkerchief flat with right side down. Bring three corners to center of cloth at bottom to resemble an envelope. Stitch edges together as close to hemmed edge of handkerchief as possible. Press seams flat and then open. Turn to right side. Fold remaining flap over opening; press envelope flat.

2. Fill in cutwork design on envelope flap as desired with metallic thread. Tack pearls in place in a pleasing arrangement.

3. Sew one button to the end of flap and a second button just below the first.

4. To make pillow, with right sides facing and raw edges aligned, use a ½-inch (1.5-cm) seam to stitch muslin pieces together, leaving a 3-inch (7.5-cm) opening in one side. Turn; then stuff pillow with fiberfill and potpourri. Tuck raw edges of fabric inside opening and stitch closed.

5. Tuck pillow inside envelope and close flap. Loop ribbon around both top and bottom buttons and tie bow.

Hope Chest

Stamped with a timeless ivy design, this graceful hope chest features traditional clean lines and minimal decoration. For best results, follow the old adage "measure twice, cut once," or simply have the wood cut at a home supply store. The pattern for the chest was designed for novice woodworkers, but if desired, you can purchase an inexpensive chest at an unfinished wood furniture store and decorate it.

- 2 pieces white pine shelving (for front and back), 23⅝ by 10 by 1 inch (60.1 by 25.5 by 2.5 cm)
- 2 pieces white pine shelving (for sides), 9¾ by 10 by 1 inch (25 by 25.5 by 2.5 cm)
- 1 piece white pine shelving (for top), 23⅝ by 11¼ by 1 inch (60.1 by 28.5 by 2.5 cm)
- 1 piece white pine shelving (for bottom), 9¾ by 22⅛ by 1 inch (25 by 56.3 by 2.5 cm)
- 2 pieces decorative molding (for front and back), 25¼ by 2 by 1 inch (64 by 5 by 2.5 cm)
- 2 pieces of decorative molding (for bottom of chest), 12¾ by 2 by 1 inch (32.5 by 5 by 2.5 cm)
- 1 pair of 1½- by 1½-inch (4- by 4-cm) surface-mounted hinges
- Four 2½-inch-diameter (6.5-cm) bunn feet, ¾-inch (2-cm) thick with screws
- Finishing nails
- Hot-glue gun and glue sticks
- Sandpaper
- Sharp handsaw
- Knife or chisel
- Electric drill
- Miter box
- Wood glue

Instructions

1. Working on a flat surface, temporarily nail the front and back pieces of the chest to the side pieces by partially driving in the nails to hold the sides together. The edges of the front and back pieces should be flush with the sides of the chest.

2. Nail the top and bottom to the sides in the same manner to ensure all edges are even.

3. If you are satisfied that all corners align evenly, disassemble the chest, then reassemble, securing with a hot-glue gun and glue sticks. When glue is dry, drive the nails all the way into the wood. Sand the outside of the chest with sandpaper.

4. Measure 2 inches (5 cm) from the top edge of the chest and draw a cutting line all the way around the perimeter of the chest. This will be the lid. Beginning at one corner, use a handsaw to cut along the cutting line. Because you will be cutting along the grain of the wood, the saw will want to follow the grain, so cut slowly and carefully.

5. Once you have sawed one side, fill the crevice with hot glue so that the cutting line will maintain a uniform space until all sawing is complete. Continue cutting the other three sides, filling the crevice with hot glue after each side is cut.

6. When finished sawing on all sides, use a sharp knife or chisel to remove the hot glue.

7. Using a drill, attach the surface-mounted hinges on the back of the chest and the lid, 3 inches (7.5 cm) in from each side.

8. Using a miter box, miter corners of all decorative molding. Using finishing nails, nail molding in place around bottom of chest.

9. Position bunn feet on all four corners of the bottom of the chest, 1 inch (2.5 cm) in from the edges; screw feet in place.

10. Paint, stencil, or decorate chest as desired and let dry.

Embossed Jewelry Box

*I*nexpensive embossed wallpaper makes a plain wooden box look as if it has been intricately carved. For best results, choose a wallpaper pattern with a noncontinuous design, so that random patterns can be cut to fit the size of the box more easily.

- Prepasted embossed wallpaper border
- Plain wooden box with hinges (available at craft stores)
- Acrylic paint: copper and white
- Clear (nonyellowing) matte varnish
- Scissors
- Sponge
- Craft knife
- Paintbrush
- Dry, clean rag
- Wood glue (optional)
- Felt (optional)

Instructions

1. Use scissors to cut out designs from the wallpaper; experiment with different shapes. Arrange wallpaper designs on the box. If the wallpaper design is narrow enough, you can fit pieces around the perimeter of the box as well as on the top as we've done here.

2. When you are pleased with your design, wet the wallpaper with a sponge and paste it to the box. Allow wallpaper to dry thoroughly.

3. If you have placed wallpaper around the edge of the box, use a craft knife to cut through the wallpaper around the opening of the box.

4. Paint box with copper paint. When copper paint is dry, apply a coat of white paint, then rub off some white paint with a dry rag to create an antiqued finish.

5. Seal box with varnish.

6. If desired, finish the inside of the box by cutting pieces of felt to the same size as the bottom and sides of the box. Secure felt pieces inside box with wood glue.

What Most Wedding Guides Don't Mention

• Most travel outside of the United States requires a passport. Applications are available from the post office on-line or from a travel agent, and there is a charge for processing the application. Two passport photographs must accompany your application. Some travel agents provide these free of charge, or photos can be made at copy centers or photography shops. It takes about four to six weeks to receive a passport; expedited service is available for a fee. If you're traveling to a Caribbean destination, a birth certificate may be an acceptable form of identification. Double-check with your travel agent when making reservations.

• Make two copies of passports, driver's licenses, and birth certificates. Tuck one copy in the bottom of your suitcase or store it in a different spot than the originals. Leave one copy at home.

These delicate, personalized brooches will become sentimental favorites
for the mothers of the bride and the groom. Choose something special for
the inside; add the frames for a finishing touch. If you craft these before the
wedding, frame a baby picture, a small love note, or flowers with special meaning. After the wedding, flowers from your bouquet, wedding snapshots, or lace
from your dress are ideal tokens of affection.

Oval Rosebud Pin *(left)*

- Brass frame charm
- Ivory paint
- Scrap of ivory card stock
- Scrap of ribbon
- Pressed flowers and greenery
- Bar pin
- Paintbrush
- Clean cloth
- Craft glue

1. To create an antiqued finish, paint the brass charm with ivory paint, then use a clean cloth to wipe charm so that paint settles only into grooves. Allow paint to dry thoroughly.

2. Place charm face down on the scrap of card stock, trace the outline of charm, then cut out design.

3. Glue ribbon to one side of card stock. Let dry, then trim around edges.

4. Arrange pressed flowers and greenery on top of ribbon. Glue dried flowers in place.

5. Frame arrangement with charm and secure with glue.

6. When glue is dry, glue bar pin to center back of charm.

Photo Frame Pin *(right)*

- 2 brass charm corners
- Ivory paint
- Photograph
- ¾-inch-square (2-cm) piece of wood or heavy cardboard
- Paintbrush
- Clean cloth
- Craft glue
- Bar pin

1. To create an antiqued finish, paint corners with ivory paint, then use a clean cloth to wipe charm so that paint settles only into grooves. Allow paint to dry thoroughly.

2. Arrange photograph diagonally on wood square or cardboard and secure with craft glue; trim around edges of photograph.

3. Position brass corners on each side of wood square so that photo is framed in the center; glue in place.

4. When glue is dry, glue bar pin to center back of charm.

Rose Petal Heart

1. Paint brass heart with red paint, then use a clean cloth to wipe charm so that paint settles only into grooves. Allow paint to dry thoroughly.

2. Place charm face down on card stock, trace the outline of charm, then cut out design.

3. Put a small amount of dried rose petals in center of heart-shaped card stock. Apply a thin line of craft glue around edges of card stock.

4. Position tulle over rose petals and press edges of tulle in place on top of line of glue. When glue is dry, trim around edges.

5. Frame rose petals with heart charm and secure with craft glue.

6. Glue rosette in center of heart.

7. When glue is dry, glue bar pin to center back of charm.

Materials

- Brass frame heart charm
- Dark red paint
- Scraps of ivory card stock
- Dried red rose petals
- Scrap of tulle
- Gold and white silk ribbon rosette
- Paintbrush
- Clean cloth
- Craft glue
- Bar pin

GIFTS FOR THE WEDDING PARTY

Forget the strand of fake pearls or the engraved shaving mug. If you really want to wow your wedding party, present them with thoughtful gifts that you'd like to receive. The best presents don't have to cost a lot of money, and they don't have to be keepsakes—but they do require a bit of forethought on your part. Here are some suggestions for great gifts.

- Pretty porcelain box with a handwritten note tucked inside
- Book of poems written by your (or the recipient's) favorite author
- Picnic basket filled with homemade gourmet foods, such as jelly, hot sauce, or flavored vinegars
- If you are the last in the group to marry, give an IOU coupon booklet for babysitting, pet watching, or cooking (possibly for an anniversary dinner).
- If you are the first of the group to marry, give each member an IOU coupon booklet for jobs you will handle for their wedding.
- Have your photographer (or someone else) take individual or couple photos and candid shots, and present photographs as gifts in a lovely frame (see page 112) or a small memory album (see page 20).
- Subscriptions to each attendant's favorite magazine
- Canvas tote or carry-all (see page 89)
- Hand-embroidered handkerchiefs
- Jewelry box (see page 32)
- Small flashlight
- Gift certificate for a manicure, car wash, or a movie
- Monogrammed pillow, towels, or pillowcases (see pages 80 and 108)
  - Engraved friendship charm
    - Swiss army knife

- Christmas ornament
- Crystal candlesticks
- Bottle of wine, a wine bag and two glasses (see pages 52 and 98)
- Wind chimes
- Garden statuary
- Handmade needlepoint pillow
- Tickets to a sporting event, play, or musical concert
- Framed photo of the wedding couple with the attendant (given after the wedding)
- Travel journal (see page 84)
- Cookbook
- Souvenir from your honeymoon
- If members of the wedding party live close by, take them to lunch individually as a thank you.
- Golf towel and golf balls
- Handsome toiletry bag
- Gift certificate for a facial, massage, or make-over
- Small painting (possibly one you painted)
- Personalized stationery
- Silk scarf or necktie
- Personalized pins (see page 34)
- Sachets (see page 24) or handmade soaps
- Host an after-the-wedding brunch to recognize everyone for their help and to share your photos, and honeymoon stories.
- Tiny pepperberry wreaths or any other small dried arrangements
- Pots of herbs, African violets, or miniature rosebushes

Tabletop Topiaries

Cut flowers last only days, but tabletop topiaries—whether dried or planted—can be enjoyed long after the wedding and reception. Use them as centerpieces at your reception, then give them as bridesmaids' gifts. If you choose a live topiary, start growing it well ahead of time, so that you can trim the topiary into the desired shape by the wedding.

Dried Herb Topiary

- 4-inch-diameter (10-cm) polystyrene ball
- Loose rosebuds, lavender, rose petals, or potpourri
- Floral foam
- 6-inch-diameter (15-cm) terra-cotta pot
- ½-inch-diameter (1.5-cm) twig, 15 inches (38 cm) long
- Spanish moss
- Ribbon (optional)
- Hot-glue gun and glue sticks

Instructions

1. Cover a small portion of the polystyrene ball with hot glue, then stick rosebuds onto ball one at a time until the entire ball is covered.

2. Cut a piece of floral foam to fit snugly inside the terra-cotta pot and wedge in place.

3. Stick the end of the twig into the bottom of the ball and the other end into the floral foam.

4. Cover the top of the floral foam with Spanish moss.

5. If desired, tie a bow around the center of the twig or around the top of the pot.

Basic Care for Live Herbal Topiaries
(see pages 40 and 41)

Light: Indoors, provide at least two hours of direct morning sun plus bright light the remainder of the day in the winter for most living herbal topiaries. Do the same in the summer, avoiding midday sun. Outdoors, provide morning sun and partial shade in the afternoon. Bring inside when the temperature drops below 40° F (4° C).

Water: Water topiaries when the surface of the dirt is dry to the touch. This can be every day if the plant is receiving adequate light. Always water thoroughly. Water slowly from the top, allowing excess water to drain. Mist the leaves of the topiary at least once a week.

Fertilizer: Feed topiary with plant food at least once a month, especially in the summer growing season.

Pruning: Regular pruning is necessary to maintain the topiary's shape. Use scissors or pruning shears to cut the plant only when necessary to keep from losing the shape.

Ivy Topiary

- Ivy plant with small leaves and long runners
- 8-inch-diameter (20.5-cm) terra-cotta pot
- Three ½-inch-diameter(1.5-cm) twigs, each 36 inches (91.5 cm) long, or a purchased metal topiary form
- Gold spray paint
- Twine

1. Repot ivy into terra-cotta pot.

2. Spray-paint twigs lightly with gold paint.

3. Wrap twine around the top of the twigs to secure, then open the twigs into a tepee shape and insert twigs into the soil in the pot, as close to the edges of the pot as possible. Wrap twine down and around the twigs into a spiral. Tie twine to twigs to secure. If you are using a metal form, position the topiary frame as desired and press into the soil.

4. Carefully wrap ivy around the twigs or metal form, tucking the ends of the ivy underneath the twine or metal as you work.

Rosemary Topiary

- Coat hanger or purchased metal topiary form
- Potted rosemary, at least 12 inches (30.5 cm) tall
- Scissors

Instructions

1. Bend the coat hanger into a circle or a heart shape and stick the hanger part down into the center of the rosemary plant. You can also purchase topiary forms in a variety of shapes.

2. Carefully begin wrapping strands of rosemary around the topiary form. When the rosemary has grown together at the top, tuck the ends of the part of the plant with new growth into the wrapped pieces of rosemary.

3. Trim as needed to train the plant into a circular or heart shape.

Going to the Chapel

"Life is the flower
for which love is the honey."

—Victor Hugo

This is the day that every young bride has waited for, that special day that changes the course of your life forever. But picture-perfect weddings don't happen by accident. They require planning, forethought, and most of all, originality.

This chapter offers a plethora of projects and plans to help you add a personal touch to either your wedding day or someone else's. Stitch a beribboned garter from scraps of lace left over from your wedding gown. With the stroke of a paintbrush, turn ordinary champagne glasses into elegant stemware ideal for toasting a new life together. Incorporate ideas from celebrations around the world into your ceremony, or become fluent in the language of flowers by studying the symbolic meanings of wedding herbs and flowers. There's something for everyone and every style in this chapter. Have fun—it's your day!

A Trio of Bridal Purses

A love letter, a tube of lipstick, a small container of aspirin—whatever you need to have on hand on your wedding day can be tucked inside one of these fancy bridal purses. You can also make multiples to give as bridesmaids' gifts. After the wedding, use the purse as a protective bag for love letters or wedding mementos—or as a travel jewelry container.

Nine-Patch Bridal Purse

Materials

- ⅓ yard (.3 m) white brocade fabric
- ¼ yard (.25 m) ivory brocade fabric
- 27 inches (68.5 cm) white satin cording with tassels
- Iron

Instructions

* *Note: Seams on bridal purses are all ½ inch (1.5 cm).*

1. From the white brocade fabric, cut a 6½- by 12½-inch (16.5- by 31.5 cm) piece for the lining; a 5- by 24-inch (12.5- by 61-cm) strip for the ruffle; and three 2½- by 10-inch (6.5- by 25.5-cm) strips for the purse.

2. From the ivory fabric, cut three 2½- by 10-inch (6.5- by 25.5-cm) strips for the purse.

3. Refer to Diagram 1 and stitch the 10-inch (25.5-cm) white and ivory strips together. Press all seams in one direction. Cut the strips into 2 ½-inch (6.5-cm) pieces.

Ivory (I)	White (W)
W	I
I	W

Diagram 1

4. Assemble strips and stitch together, using Diagram 2 as a guide. Press all seams in one direction.

I	W	I	W	I	W
W	I	W	I	W	I
I	W	I	W	I	W

Diagram 2

5. Fold pieced fabric for purse in half lengthwise. With right sides together and raw edges aligned, stitch sides and bottom together. Press seams open. Stitch edges of lining together in the same way.

6. Turn purse inside out. Insert lining into purse with wrong sides of purse and lining together and seams and top edges aligned.

7. Fold ruffle piece in half so that right sides are together and short ends are aligned; stitch short ends together. Turn to right side and press seam open.

8. Fold ruffle piece in half so that right sides are together and long raw edges are aligned; stitch long edges together.

9. Stitch along ruffle twice, once ½ inch (1.5 cm) from raw edges and once ¼ inch (.5 cm) from edges. Pull threads to ruffle, easing and adjusting length to fit around top of purse.

10. With right sides together and raw edges aligned, pin ruffle in place to top edge of outside of bag, then stitch. Press seam to inside.

11. Turn edge of lining down to cover raw edges of ruffle and blindstitch in place.

12. Position cording on seam as shown in photograph and whipstitch cording in place, leaving enough free to tie.

Pink Velvet Purse

⅓ yard (.3 m) pink velvet
⅓ yard (.3 m) white polyester jacquard fabric
Paper plate

4-inch-diameter (10-cm) decorative lace flower
24 inches (61 cm) flat braid, white
30 inches (76 cm) white satin cording, ¼ inch (.5 cm) wide

1. Cut two 7- by 10½-inch (18- by 26.5-cm) pieces from velvet; cut two pieces from the lining fabric (jacquard) to the same measurements.

2. Stack fabrics on top of each other, then position paper plate over fabric, aligning the curve of the plate with the bottom edges of the fabric pieces. Mark curve, then cut along markings to create the bottom curve of the purse.

3. With right sides together and raw edges aligned, stitch velvet pieces together, leaving top (uncurved) end open. Press seams open and turn to right side. Stitch lining pieces together using the same method.

4. Tack decorative lace flower to one side of velvet bag; use photograph as a guide for positioning flower.

5. Insert lining into bag, making sure wrong sides of lining and purse are facing. Fold seams to the inside, aligning edges. Blindstitch lining to bag.

6. Hand-stitch flat braid along the top edge of bag and along bottom front of bag.

7. Fold piece of cording in half, then tack center of cording to center back of bag, 2 inches (5 cm) from the top edge. Bring cording to front and tie into a bow. Knot ends.

Drawstring Bag

Materials

½ yard (.45 m) white damask

½ yard (.45 m) ivory damask

8-inch-diameter (20.5-cm) round Battenberg lace doily

2 yards white satin cording, ¼ inch (.5 cm) wide

Sewing machine

Clear tape

Safety pin

Instructions

1. Cut a 14-inch-diameter (35.5-cm) circle from both the white and ivory fabrics.

2. To make holes for the drawstring, measure 2½ inches (6.5 cm) in from the edge of the ivory circle on opposite sides of the circle. Stitch 1-inch (2.5-cm) buttonholes. Slit buttonholes.

3. Center doily on ivory circle, then tack doily in place along edges.

4. With right sides together and raw edges aligned, stitch circles together, leaving a 3-inch (7.5-cm) opening for turning. Press, turn, and stitch opening closed.

5. Beginning at top of buttonhole, stitch around the circle, 2½ inches (6.5 cm) from the edge. Stitch around circle again 1 inch (2.5 cm) from first stitching line to form a channel for the cording. The buttonhole openings should fall between the edge of the circle and the stitching line.

6. For drawstrings, cut cording in half; finish ends of cording with tape to prevent raveling. Use safety pin to thread one piece of cording around circle through one buttonhole; thread remaining cording around circle through other buttonhole. Knot ends of cords together at each buttonhole opening, then trim tape from the ends. Pull drawstrings to gather and close purse.

PICTURE PERFECT

It is said that a picture is worth a thousand words, and nothing could be more true when it comes to wedding pictures. The most important ingredient in good wedding photography is the photographer. But there are several things you can do and suggest that will make a difference in the outcome of your photos.

• Choose a photographer by looking through his or her portfolio. If you really like a friend's wedding photographs, look at pictures of people you don't know to make sure you're really impressed with the photographer and not emotionally attached to the people in the photographs.

• If you opt for formal, portrait-quality photos, have a friend who is a good amateur photographer take candid shots before and after the wedding. Candid photographs often capture the feeling of the day more accurately than posed pictures.

• If possible, have photos taken in both black-and-white and color film. Color shows a realistic setting; black-and-white film creates classic photos that won't look dated in twenty years.

• For an old-fashioned look, take black-and-white photographs and have them hand-colored.

• When deciding which shots you'd like the photographer to take, think of your wedding as a story. What elements are important to the story line? What photos will capture your personality? What photos will show your future children what it was like to be there on your wedding day?

• To get a cost estimate, you'll need to know the size of your wedding, the length of time you would like the photographer to be there, and whether the wedding will be held indoors or outdoors. If the photographer's rates fall within your budget, schedule a time to review his or her portfolio.

• The best photographers are creative. That means that, although they can take quality photographs, they also have the ability to make each wedding look unique. When reviewing a portfolio, ask yourself if each wedding looks the same, or if they stand apart from each other.

• Choose a photographer you like. If you have trouble communicating with someone before the wedding, you'll certainly have trouble on your wedding day.

• Choose an acid-free album for storing your photographs.

• Have a professional video made. Videos will tell the story very differently from photography, and you'll want to have images of your wedding in as many formats as possible.

• Ask if you can have images on disc so you can create a web site or e-mail photos to friends who were unable to attend the ceremony.

• Ask the photographer if you can buy the negatives after a certain length of time.

Keepsake Handkerchief Bonnet

This pretty, keepsake handkerchief does double duty when you turn it into a baby bonnet. For the wedding, you can carry the handkerchief as a token of something new. When your first child is born, the handkerchief can be quickly stitched into a precious bonnet for your baby's christening.

Materials

- 12-inch-square (30.5-cm) handkerchief with lace edges
- 3 silk ribbon rosettes, white
- 24 inches (61 cm) picot ribbon, ¼ inch (.5 cm) wide
- Iron

Instructions:

1. Press handkerchief flat.

2. To create the front section of the bonnet, make a 2-inch (5-cm) fold back onto handkerchief.

3. To create the back section of the bonnet, make a 4-inch (10-cm) accordion fold back onto handkerchief, then make another 2-inch (5-cm) accordion fold toward the back. (Lace edges should face to back side of bonnet.)

4. To complete the bonnet, overlap back corners (the double-folded section), and tack corners together through all layers. Stitch one rosette over tacking.

5. Loop one edge of ribbon as shown in photograph, then stitch base of loop to the center of the front fold on one side of the bonnet, just above the edge of the lace. Tack rosette over stitching, catching all layers. Repeat step 5 on other side of bonnet.

Heirloom Flower Girl's Collar

ine fabric, exquisite handwork, and dainty bead embellishments give this collar a trea-
sured, heirloom quality—it will be your secret how simple it is to make! We used a 10-inch-
square (25.5-cm) cocktail napkin, but a large crocheted doily, a fine handkerchief, or a round table
scarf work just as well. Make sure the piece of fabric is large enough to drape over the shoulders and
across the front and back of the flower girl's dress.

- Antique linen napkin, handkerchief, or table scarf
- Scrap of coordinating fabric (for bias strip)
- Beaded lace trim (quantity will vary)
- Small button
- Iron

1. Press the fabric flat.

2. Using a purchased pattern or the neck measurement of the flower girl as a guide, cut a neck opening in the center of the fabric.

3. Fold fabric diagonally, then cut a slit from the neck opening down one side to make a placket; stop 1½ inches (4 cm) from the point of the fabric.

4. Cut a 1-inch (2.5-cm) bias strip from coordinating fabric (see page 11). A bias strip is cut diagonally across the grain of the fabric. To cut the bias strip, measure the neck hole and placket edges to determine the length of the bias strip needed. Add 2 inches (5 cm) to allow for overlap. Cut bias strips 2 inches (5 cm) wide and the length of the determined measurements.

5. Baste around neck opening. With right sides together and raw edges aligned, hand-stitch bias strip around slit; turn, press to wrong side of collar, then turn raw edges under and stitch in place. Stitch ends of bias strip under to finish.

6. Hand-stitch beaded lace around the neck edge; turn ends of lace under at placket and hand-stitch to finish.

7. Add closure to collar by tacking a button at the top of collar slit, then making a matching loop of thread.

Wedding Celebrations Around the World

- Pope Innocent III decreed that there be a waiting period between betrothal and marriage. Thus began the custom of wearing two rings, one for the engagement and one for the wedding.

- In some cultures, legend has it that after the first wedding in a family, a portion of the cake must be kept in the house until all daughters are married; this is to keep the unwed daughters from becoming old maids.

- British brides carry a lump of sugar in their bodices to assure sweetness throughout their marriage.

- People of the Jewish faith have a wedding tradition of breaking of glass as a reminder of the destruction of the Holy Temple in Jerusalem. A wine glass is wrapped in a handkerchief or napkin and placed on the ground for the groom to stomp and smash. The custom also signifies the close of the marriage ceremony.

- In Peru, the wedding party decorates the honeymoon bed with red and green chili peppers to assure a fruitful and passionate marriage.

Easy Etched Stemware

Though it may seem as if etching would require advanced crafting skills, this technique is really quite easy to master. All you do is apply etching paste to glass using a precut pattern. For the pattern, use stencil designs or patterns from gift wrap or magazines that have distinct outer edges and no small, intricate lines running throughout the pattern. You can also use the fleur-de-lis pattern provided.

Materials

- Paper with adhesive backing
- Purchased champagne glasses
- Etching creme
- Pencil
- Craft knife
- Spatula
- Plastic container large enough to cover champagne glass (for etched glass with clear design only)

Instructions

1. First, trace the chosen design on adhesive-backed paper. Use a craft knife to cut around design about 1 inch (2.5 cm) from the outside edge of the design.

2. Remove paper backing and position design on glass. Smooth adhesive paper flat against glass with a spatula. Make sure all bubbles and wrinkles are smoothed out.

3. To create an etched design on clear glass, cut around the outside edge of the design, then cut a slit down the center of the design with a craft knife. Using the tip of the craft knife, carefully lift the inside of the design from the glass. Smooth the edges of the adhesive paper against the glass with a spatula. Carefully apply etching creme over the clear cutout in the adhesive paper. Do not drip or spill etching creme on any other part of the glass, as it will cloud the glass.

4. To create an etched glass with a clear design, cut around the outside edge of the design. Using the craft knife, carefully lift the adhesive paper around the design from the glass, leaving the adhesive design intact. Smooth the edges of the adhesive design against the glass with a spatula. Pour the etching creme into a plastic container, then dip the glass into the creme.

5. Leave creme on glass for 15 minutes, then dab off excess with a clean rag. Rinse with cold water. Do not allow creme that is rinsing off to run onto the bare glass. Remove the paper design from the glass.

Flower Girl Basket

This dainty whitewashed basket is adorned with leaves, creamy white dahlia heads, baby's breath, and beautiful ribbons. All you need are flowers, ribbon, and a hot-glue gun. You may want to craft several additional baskets to use as table decorations.

- 2 yards (1.8 m) white satin ribbon, ⅛ inch (.3 cm) wide
- Whitewashed wicker basket
- 1 bunch dried baby's breath/gypsophilia
- 2 stems dried salal leaves
- 2 yards (2.7 m) white sheer ribbon, 1⅜ inch (3.5 cm) wide
- 14 cream-colored dried dahlia heads
- 1 yard (.9 m) white sheer ribbon with scalloped edge, ½ inch (1.5 cm) wide
- Hot-glue gun and glue sticks

Instructions

1. Cut two 1-yard (.9-m) lengths of ⅛-inch (.3 cm) satin ribbon. Using the photograph as a guide, wrap the basket handle with satin ribbon in a crisscross pattern. Secure ribbon in place on handle with hot glue.

2. Hot-glue sprigs of baby's breath around the entire upper edge of the basket.

3. Hot-glue a row of salal leaves on top of the baby's breath around the edge of the basket.

4. Loop a yard (.9 m) of 1⅜-inch (3.5-cm) sheer ribbon along the side of basket and between leaves as shown in the photograph and hot-glue in place.

5. Attach dahlia heads to the basket between the leaves and the ribbon loops with hot glue.

6. Tie a bow with the two thicknesses of sheer ribbon and attach the bow at base of the handle on one side of the basket.

Wedding Celebrations Around the World

- White is the most common color for a wedding dress in Western culture, but, until recently, Icelandic brides wore black velvet wedding dresses embroidered with silver and gold. Red, the color of love and joy, is often worn by Chinese brides.

- Fertility symbols have always been prevalent in wedding celebrations. Even today, many of our customs are remnants of these ancient beliefs. For example, silver coins were first placed in the bride's shoe to appease Diana, the goddess of chastity and unmarried maidens, so that she would allow the bride to lose her virginity and bear a child. A bouquet of flowers symbolizes life, growth, and fertility.

- Showering a newly married couple with food signifies hope that the couple will be as fruitful as the earth. Americans traditionally throw rice, the French shower wheat on the couple, and in England, pieces of cake are thrown.

Party Favors

If good things come in small packages, then your guests will be delighted to receive these hand-crafted party favors. Though you have plenty of ideas to choose from, these small tokens of affection share the same purpose: to say thank you to the friends and family members who participate in your special day.

Ornament Elegance. Even if your wedding does not happen around the holidays, you can still give holiday ornaments as wedding favors. If you pile them together in an antique urn or hand-painted basket, they become a one-of-a-kind table centerpiece. To make this ornament, we filled a clear plastic ball with baby's breath and a length of pearl cording—loose beads, confetti, and bits of lace and ribbon work just as well. Top the ornament off by tying a bow around the top and adding a ribbon for a hanger. ▼

Love Letters. Say thank you with small envelopes fashioned from gold-flecked handmade paper. Knot a piece of gold cording, fringe the ends, and glue cording to the center of the envelope. Tuck a piece of tissue paper and a tiny trinket or piece of candy inside.

Miniature Flowerpots. These planted blooms make great gifts for your wedding guests. Purchase small pots at a local nursery or craft store, then paint and decorate pots as desired. Buy small six-packs of flowers and repot single flowers into pots. During the reception, you can use groupings of the potted flowers as centerpieces and interior decorations. If you'd rather not bother with live plants, insert envelopes filled with seeds into each pot. Your guests can then take the seeds home and plant their own flowers as a remembrance of your wedding.

Scented Sachets. Muslin tea bags make ideal casings for old-fashioned scented sachets. To paint the outside of the bag, insert a heavy piece of cardboard inside to keep the paint from seeping through. Draw a monogrammed letter, fleur-de-lis, or any other motif on the outside, then fill in with paint. When the paint is dry, fill the bag with potpourri and gather the strings to close the bag.

Handcrafted Candles. These rolled beeswax candles are quick and easy to create and make impressive wedding favors. Choose your favorite color of beeswax, then cut the sheets to the desired size. Fold and press the edge of one side of the beeswax sheet over the wick, then begin rolling the sheet into a candle. Trim the wick, leaving about 1¼ inches (3 cm) at the top. For fatter candles, roll several sheets together. For candles with a swirled appearance, cut the beeswax sheet on the diagonal before rolling. If desired, wrap a thank-you note around the candle and finish with a bow.

Transparent Envelopes. Small envelopes are the perfect packaging for wrapping gold chocolate coins, sugar-coated almonds, or potpourri. Using the diagram as a guide (see Paper Pockets below), make an envelope out of a sheet of acetate. Insert a paper doily, add your goodies, and seal the envelope with a pretty sticker.

Tokens in Tulle. Update traditional rice bags by filling them with potpourri instead of birdseed. Cut the tulle into 8-inch-diameter (20.5 cm) circles, fill with potpourri, and tie with raffia. For extra decoration, tuck a tiny flower or small wedding trinket into the knot.

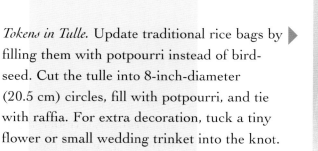

Petal Pins. Small boutonnieres and corsages make each guest feel part of the wedding festivities. For practical purposes, use dried or faux flowers, but if you have time, fresh flowers also work nicely. Simply cut flower stems to about 3 inches (7.5 cm) in length, then wrap flower ends with narrow satin ribbon. Secure the ends of ribbon with clear tape or hot glue. If desired, tie wire-edged bows around the stems. Stick a floral pin through each stem. Display the flowers together by sticking the stems in a large moss-covered foam base or by pinning them to swaths of satin ribbon and tulle.

Lacy Heart Sachet. Add a loop so your guests can hang these lovely sachets from a doorknob or any other spot. To make the sachet, embellish two lacy heart appliqués with gold beads. Stitch the appliqués together, inserting a tulle packet filled with lavender seed. Finish by tacking a bow and ribbon at the top of the sachet for a hanger.

Silver Bells. Instead of throwing birdseed or flower petals, have your guests ring miniature silver bells when you and your groom leave the wedding. Begin by threading several 7-inch (18-cm) lengths of thin wire through the top of purchased silver bells (available at craft stores). Form a loop with the wire by twisting the ends together. If you wish, wrap ribbon tightly around wire, completely covering the loop. Embellish with bows and faux flowers.

Paper Pockets. Fine paper can be folded into attractive pockets that are just the right size for cookies, gold chocolate coins, or handwritten thank-yous. To make the pockets, choose a heavyweight paper. Cut the paper into a 3½- by 12-inch (9- by 30.5-cm) piece. Using the diagram as a guide, form a pocket by folding three sides of the paper inward; cut off the top triangular piece from the pocket. Glue the folded sides of the pocket together to secure, then glue ribbon around edges of pocket to finish.

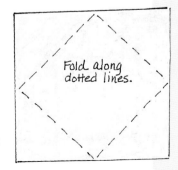

Fold along dotted lines.

Stylish Wedding Gloves

*W*hy pay an exorbitant price for lacy gloves when you can make a one-of-a-kind set for much less? Use scraps of trim and pearls from your dress or choose lace appliqués to match. The two styles featured here require minimal stitching.

Gloves with Rosettes and Pearls

Materials

(for two gloves)

- Purchased gloves
- Two 10-inch (25.5-cm) pieces of 1-inch-wide (2.5-cm) tulle trim with pearl rope
- 2 satin ribbon rosettes

Instructions

1. Fold piece of tulle in half to determine center. Position center of trim over center of glove front and over seam line around edge of glove. Pin in place.

2. Carefully tack trim to glove at each juncture of tulle and pearl rope and trim excess. Position rosette over trim ends and tack rosette to glove. Repeat steps to make second glove.

Lace and Pearl Gloves

Materials

(for two gloves)

- Purchased gloves
- 2 lace appliqués
- Small white pearls

Instructions

1. When choosing an appliqué, take the gloves with you. Try appliqués on gloves until you find a size, texture, and color that is appropriate for your gloves. (If you are embellishing long gloves, you may want to use more than one appliqué.) The appliqué should be complementary to the lace of the gown or dress. You may also be able to cut a motif from heavy corded bridal lace and stitch to gloves.

2. First, lay appliqué on back of glove to determine placement. (Refer to the photograph for suggested placement.) Pin appliqué in place.

3. Carefully tack appliqué to glove, stitching around the outer edges of the appliqué. Stitch pearls to appliqué for embellishment. Repeat steps to make second glove.

Keepsake Garter

*S*omething old, something new, something borrowed, something blue.... A touch of blue accents this frilly garter. Start with a length of organdy, then add lace, pearls, ribbons, and a flower to create a dainty wedding accessory.

- Pearl-trimmed lace, ½ inch (1.5 cm) wide
- Lace in coordinating color, ½ inch (1.5 cm) wide
- Flat lace, 1 inch (2.5 cm) wide
- 2 pieces of organdy, 2 inches (5 cm) wide
- Elastic, ¼ inch (.5 cm) wide (amount will vary — see below)
- Two 12-inch (30.5-cm) lengths white ribbon, ⅛ inch (.3 cm) wide
- 12 inches (30.5 cm) blue ribbon, ⅛ inch (.3 cm) wide
- White silk flower
- Safety pin
- Iron
- Sewing machine

Note: Amounts of materials will vary, depending on the bride's measurement.

Instructions

1. Before you begin, measure around the bride's leg, just above the knee. Multiply this measurement by one-and-a-half. This is the length of organdy and lace needed for the garter. All seams are ½ inch (1.5 cm).

2. Stitch pearl-trimmed and coordinating lace along long sides of one piece of organdy.

3. With right sides together and raw edges aligned, stitch organdy pieces together along long edges, catching lace in seams. Turn and press.

4. Position flat lace in center of organdy and machine-stitch on both sides of lace to make a ½-inch (1.5-cm) tunnel for the elastic.

5. Use a safety pin to thread elastic through the tunnel. Add ½ inch (1.5 cm) to bride's leg measurement for amount of elastic needed.

6. With right sides together and raw edges aligned, stitch short sides of garter together, catching elastic in seam. Trim elastic and fold raw edges of organdy under; blindstitch folded edges in place.

7. Using the photograph as a guide, make loops with the remaining ribbons and tack ribbons to garter. Tack silk flower on top of ribbons.

Elegant Hair Accessories

Present your bridesmaids and flower girl with elegant hair accessories to wear in the wedding and to keep as a lovely reminder of the day. Quick and easy to make, these accessories can be matched to the colors of your wedding. You may even want to make some extras to coordinate with clothes you plan to take along on your honeymoon.

Satin Scrunchie

~ 2-inch-diameter (5-cm) elastic hair band
~ 10 yards (9.15 m) ivory satin ribbon, ⅛ inch (.3 cm) wide
~ Crochet hook, size 9 or I

1. Loop yarn over the elastic band, then crochet five chain stitches. To crochet a chain stitch, begin by making a loop. Make a slip knot near the end of the thread. Hold the loop between the thumb and the forefinger of one hand. Hold the hook in the opposite hand. Insert hook in the loop and pull up close around end of hook (not too tight). Pass the hook under the thread and catch the thread with the hook. This is called "thread over." Draw thread through the loop on the hook. This makes one chain stitch. Do not pull tight.

2. Single-crochet inside the elastic band, then crochet five chain stitches. To crochet a single crochet stitch, insert the hook from the front under the two top threads of the chain stitch. Catch the thread with the hook (thread over, see step 1) and draw the thread through the stitch. There should now be two loops on the hook. Thread over again and draw the thread through the two loops. One loop remains on the hook. This completes one single crochet.

3. Repeat steps 1 and 2 until you reach the end of the ribbon. Pull end of ribbon through the first chain and tie off.

Rosebud Barrette

~ Tulle, 6 by 1½ inches (15 by 4 cm)
~ Metal barrette, 2¾ inches (7 cm) in length
~ 1 yard (.9) ivory satin ribbon, ⅛ inch (.3 cm) wide
~ Dried rosebuds (exact number will vary, depending on size of rosebuds.)
~ Sewing machine
~ Hot-glue gun and glue sticks

1. Machine-stitch down the center of the tulle. Do not backstitch at beginning or end or cut thread ends. Locate bobbin thread (thread on bottom) and carefully pull to gather tulle. Continue to pull gathering threads to adjust tulle to the length of the barrette. Hot-glue tulle to barrette.

2. Beginning at one end of barrette, loop ribbon from side to side to end of barrette, securing ribbon with hot glue as you go. With remainder of ribbon, make a tiny bow; trim excess ends.

3. Arrange rosebuds along the top of the barrette—on top of the tulle and the ribbon loops. Secure rosebuds with hot glue. Glue bow at the hinge end of the barrette.

Golden Rosette Headband *(see page 64)*

— White headband (Measure before cutting and make adjustments to ribbon as needed.)

— 15 inches (38 cm) white scalloped-edged ribbon, ¾ inch (2 cm) wide

— 15 inches (38 cm) gold and white ribbon with rosettes, ⅛ inch (.3 cm) wide

— Hot-glue gun and glue sticks

Instructions

1. Glue white ribbon on outside of headband; trim ribbon ends and turn ribbon under on each end to hide raw edges.

2. Glue rosette ribbon on top of white ribbon; turn ends under on each end to hide raw edges.

Pearl and Ribbon Headband *(see page 64)*

— White headband (Measure before cutting and make adjustments to ribbon as needed.)

— 15 inches (38 cm) ivory tulle with pearl trim

— 15 inches (38 cm) ivory satin ribbon, ⅛ inch (.3 cm) wide

— 2 ribbon rosettes, ivory

— Hot-glue gun and glue sticks

Instructions

1. Cover outside of headbead with tulle and pearl trim and secure to headband with hot glue.

2. Wrap ribbon around headband and over trim. Secure ribbon in spots with hot glue.

3. To finish, trim ends of tulle and ribbon, and glue ribbon rosette at each end of headband.

THE LANGUAGE OF FLOWERS

radition, fragrance, and beauty are obvious reasons to carry a bridal bouquet; but if you want to make every gesture count, then choose flowers with meanings that represent appropriate virtues or sentiments.

The language of flowers is centuries old and began with herbs that had ancient symbolic meanings in Chinese, Greek, Roman, Turkish, and Egyptian cultures. In the early 1600s, John Parkinson, a French herbalist and physician, gave meaning to diminutive nosegays of fragrant flowers and leaves. The tradition continued and by the Victorian era, the art of sending symbolic messages by gifts of flowers, called *floriography*, was all the rage.

Flowers and Foliage

Daisy	Innocence
Fern	Fascination, sincerity
Forget-me-not	True love
Honeysuckle	Faithfulness
Ivy	Fidelity, marriage, and friendship
Lavender	Devotion
Lily of the valley	Purity, peace, and return of happiness
Orchid	Beauty
Rose	Love and unity
Violet	Faith and loyalty
White Carnation	Remembrance

Herbs and Spices

Basil	Love, spice of life, good wishes
Bay	Glory
Coriander	Hidden worth
Cloves	Dignity
Dianthus	Bonds of affection
Goldenrod	Encouragement
Lemon Balm	Sympathy
Lemon Verbena	Enchantment
Parsley	Festivity
Peppermint	Warmth of feeling
Rosemary	Remembrance, fidelity
Sage	Long life and good health

Floral Pew Marker

*F*lowers are among the most expensive wedding purchases. This quick, easy, and inexpensive arrangement makes a lovely pew marker while helping you trim your floral budget. You can either purchase dried flowers or save cuttings from your garden throughout the year.

Another money- and time-saving tip: ask your florist for flower heads that have fallen off the stems. These blooms, which would have been discarded by the florist, can be incorporated easily into your dried arrangements.

Materials

- 1 yard (.9 m) white, wired-edged satin ribbon, ¾ inch (2 cm) wide
- 6-inch-diameter (15-cm) polystyrene ball, cut in halves
- 1 stem dried baby's breath/gypsophilia
- 1 stem dried salal leaves
- Cream-colored dahlia heads, approximately 24
- 1½ yards (1.4 m) wire-edged, white sheer ribbon, 1½ inch (4 cm) wide
- Hot-glue gun and glue sticks
- Floral wire

Instructions

1. Hot-glue satin ribbon around outside (bottom) edge of one half of the foam ball, leaving a 6-inch (15-cm) loop at one end for a hanger, and 3-inch (7.5-cm) tails at the other end.

2. Beginning just above the edge of the satin ribbon, hot-glue sprigs of gypsophilia around edge of ball.

3. Hot-glue a layer of salal leaves on top of gypsophilia around edge of ball. Gypsophilia should show under the edges of the leaves.

4. Hot-glue a second row of gypsophilia above salal leaves, then fill in the center of the ball with dahlia heads.

5. Tie a bow with the sheer ribbon and attach bow to base of hanger with floral wire.

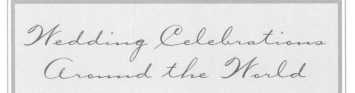

Wedding Celebrations Around the World

• Gold rings were circulated as currency in ancient Egypt. When a man gave a woman his ring, it meant that he trusted her with his property. Under Roman law, the ring was a sign of security. In the 1800s, the diamond ring—symbolizing innocence, matrimonial happiness, wealth, and everlasting devotion—became popular for engagements.

• Wedding bands are worn on the third finger of the left hand because of an ancient Egyptian belief that a vein ran from that finger directly to the heart. Another belief, dating back to the 17th century, is that, during a Christian wedding, a priest would get to the fourth finger (counting the thumb) after touching the first three fingers and saying, "in the name of the Father, the Son, and the Holy Ghost."

Ring Bearer's Pillow

*Y*ou can either make this ring bearer's pillow out of fabric scraps or simply embellish a purchased pillow. Try personalizing the pillow by embroidering your initials and the date of your wedding on top. When a sister or close friend gets married, pass the pillow along. To create a lasting family heirloom, embroider the relevant initials and wedding date next to your own.

- 1 yard (.9 m) pearl edge trim
- 2 pieces of ivory linen, each 9 inches (23 cm) square
- 2 lace corner appliqués, each approximately 6 inches (15 cm) wide
- Small white pearls, approximately 100
- 2½-inch (6.5-cm) lace heart appliqués
- 5 yards (4.5 m) white satin ribbon, ⅛ inch (.3 cm) wide
- 2 yards (1.8 m) white wire-edged ribbon, 1½ inches (4 cm) wide
- Fiberfill stuffing

Instructions

Note: All seams are ½ inch (1.5 cm).

1. Stitch pearl trim around edges of one square of the white linen.

2. With right sides together and raw edges aligned, stitch linen squares together, catching trim in seam. Leave opening for turning. Clip corners, press, and turn.

3. Using the photograph as a guide, position corner lace appliqués on opposite corners of one side of the pillow, aligning ends, and stitch in place. Sew pearls on lace as desired.

4. Position lace heart appliqué in the center of the pillow, tack in place, and embellish with pearls.

5. Cut white satin ribbon to 12-, 18-, and 36-inch (30.5-, 45.5-, and 91.5-cm) lengths.

6. Tie one bow with both the 36-inch (91.5-cm) piece of ribbon and the 12-inch (30.5-cm) piece. Fold 18-inch (45.5-cm) ribbon in half, center on top of heart appliqué, and tack in place along fold line. Tack bow on top of ribbon.

7. For bows on corners of pillow, make two bows, using 1 yard (.9 m) of the wire-edged ribbon for each bow.

8. Cut two each 24-, 18-, and 12-inch (61-, 45.5-, and 30.5-cm) lengths of ⅛-inch (.3-cm) satin ribbon. Make Lark's head knots (see page 10) around wire bow centers, using 24-inch (61-cm) lengths of ribbon. Thread the 18- and 12-inch (45.5- and 30.5-cm) lengths through the loops of the Lark's head knots.

9. Tack the bows to opposite corners of the pillow.

Magic Slippers

*D*ress up plain dyeable shoes for your wedding with lace, ribbon, and ribbon rosettes. These gorgeous slippers will look great peeking out from under the wedding gown and bridesmaids' dresses. You can also embellish Mom's shoes to match her dress. For a simpler approach, decorate only the heels or the toes.

(for embellishing toe and heel of both shoes)

- Satin dyeable shoes
- Two 6-inch (15-cm) pieces of scalloped-edged white ribbon, ½ inch (1.5 cm) wide
- Two 6-inch (15-cm) pieces of white satin ribbon, ⅛ inch (.3 cm) wide (for heels)
- Two 1-inch (2.5-cm) white ribbon rosettes
- 2 white lace appliqués
- Two 3-inch (7.5-cm) pieces of white satin ribbon, ⅛ inch (.3 cm) wide (for toes)
- Two ½-inch (1.5-cm) white ribbon rosettes
- Fabric glue

Instructions

1. To embellish heel, fold one 6-inch (15-cm) length of ½-inch-wide (1.5-cm) ribbon in half. Position the center of ribbon at the top edge of the heel and glue in place.

2. Fold a 6-inch (15-cm) length of ⅛-inch (.3 cm) satin ribbon in half. Position center of narrow ribbon at the top edge of back of heel, allowing center loop to extend approximately ½ inch (1.5 cm) above the edge of shoe; glue in place.

3. Position ribbon rosette on top of ribbon lengths and glue in place. Trim ends of ribbon as needed. Repeat steps 1 through 3 for other shoe.

4. To embellish the toe, center heart appliqués on the toe of one shoe, allowing top edges of appliqués to extend over edge of shoe slightly. Lightly glue with fabric glue. Referring to photograph for placement, fold ⅛-inch (.3-cm) satin ribbon in half and glue to appliqué. Glue ½-inch (1.5-cm) rosette on top of ribbon. Repeat step 4 for other shoe.

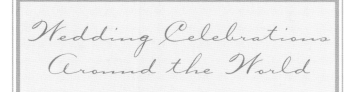

Wedding Celebrations Around the World

- White wedding gowns were first worn by Victorian brides to indicate that they were wealthy enough to wear a dress only once. But even when white came to symbolize purity, the dresses were often worn more than once. In the early 20th century, brides wore their wedding dresses on special occasions throughout the first year of marriage.

- "Something old, something new, something borrowed, something blue . . ." This familiar wedding custom is steeped in tradition. Something old signifies continuity, a bridge between the bride's old life and her new one. The bride might wear a piece of jewelry from her mother or grandmother. Something new represents good fortune, success, and hope for the future. A bride's wedding dress can represent something new. Something borrowed should be lent from a happily married friend in hopes that the happiness will rub off. This could be jewelry or an item of clothing. Something blue denotes purity, fidelity, and love. Today, the garter is often trimmed in blue.

Damask Tablecloth

This lovely tablecloth can be draped over the wedding party's table at the reception, then the couple can use it later for a romantic dinner or an elegant brunch. Use purchased linens to make the cloth or make the tablecloth extra special by stitching together your grandmother's antique linens. The size can be varied based on the size and number of napkins used.

(for a 36-inch-square [91.5-cm] tablecloth)

– 4 white damask or linen napkins, 18 inches (45.5 cm) square

– 2 yards (1.9 m) white satin ribbon, ½ inch (1.5 cm) wide

– 8-inch-diameter (20.5-cm) white crocheted doily

– 4½ yards (4.2 m) white lace trim, 1 inch (2.5 cm) wide (or enough for the perimeter of the tablecloth)

– Sewing machine

1. Position the edges of two napkins parallel to each other so that they are touching, then zigzag-stitch across edges of both napkins to secure pieces together. Repeat step 1 with the two remaining napkins.

2. Align the two sets of stitched napkins to make a square and zigzag-stitch pieces together in the same manner as step 1.

3. To cover seams, cut satin ribbon to fit over zigzag seams, position ribbon along seams, then stitch ribbons to tablecloth.

4. Place doily in center of the square, pin, and stitch to square cloth approximately 2 inches (5 cm) from the outside edge of the doily. Repeat stitching again ¼ inch (.5 cm) from first line of stitching. Zigzag-stitch around outside edge of doily.

5. Turn tablecloth to the wrong side and carefully trim center of tablecloth away along stitching line on doily.

6. Stitch lace trim to outside edge of tablecloth.

"We love because it's the only true adventure."

—Nikki Giovanni

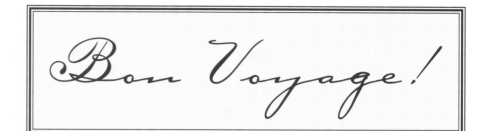

Bon Voyage!

ecause the wedding itself requires an exorbitant amount of time and energy, honeymoon plans can sometimes be an afterthought. But what a sweet afterthought it is! This is your chance to relax and enjoy the beginning of your new life together.

In this chapter, you'll find everything you need to set sail for an idyllic honeymoon. Stitch a handy honeymoon travel set to carry your trousseau or craft a travel journal to record your special honeymoon memories. For relieving stress and rejuvenating your body and spirit after the wedding, make bath salts and lotions to take with you on your trip. And if you can't take an extended vacation after your wedding, you'll find lots of unique alternatives and suggestions for enjoying a delightful honeymoon at home.

Bon Voyage Basket

*S*ometimes receptions get so hectic that the bride and groom do not get a chance to sample any of the food. For a sweet send-off, fill this elegant basket with goodies from the reception and tuck the basket into the back seat of the couple's car. Once the food is gone, the basket can be used as a picnic basket or as a decorative home accessory.

Note: Fabric requirements will vary based on the size of basket you use. This basket is 20 inches (51 cm) long, 12 inches (30.5 cm) wide, and 7 inches (18 cm) deep.

- Basket
- Two coordinating fabrics (We used a cotton homespun and a quilt print.)
- 4 yards (3.7 m) cording with knitted lip (for sewing into seam), ½ inch (1.5 cm) thick

Instructions

1. To determine the amount of fabric required, measure the bottom width, the bottom length, and the depth of the basket. Add twice the depth plus the width plus 4 inches (10 cm) to determine the width of fabric needed. Add four times the depth plus the length to determine the length of fabric needed. Use these measurements to cut out pieces from both types of fabric.

2. Lay the fabric diagonally in the basket with the longer end draping over the ends of the basket and the points of the shorter side in line with the handle. Adjust the fabric so that you have a 2-inch (5-cm) overlap along the outside edges of the length of the basket. Measure and trim corners away to make room for placing ties at handle. (Use the diagram as a guide.)

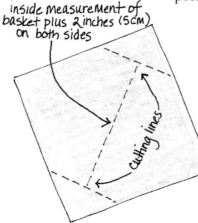

inside measurement of basket plus 2 inches (5cm) on both sides

cutting lines

3. Find the center of length of the fabric. This center mark is where the fabric will be tied around the handle of the basket. From this center mark, measure 1½ inches (4 cm) from either side. This is where you will begin and end the cording. Mark both sides of fabric for cording/tie placement.

4. Beginning at one 1½-inch (4-cm) mark, leaving a 12-inch (30.5-cm) tail of cord, stitch cord around to fabric to the first 1½-inch (4 cm) mark on the other side of the fabric. Leave a 12-inch (30.5-cm) tail of cording. Repeat this step, beginning at the second 1½-inch (4-cm) mark, beginning and ending with a 12-inch (30.5-cm) tail of cord. This 3-inch (7.5 cm) spacing on either side is where the cloth is tied around the basket handle. Press and clip seams as needed.

5. To make ties, remove the knitted lip from the cording up to the fabric stitching. Knot ends of cording and fringe or trim as desired.

6. With right sides together and raw edges aligned, stitch fabrics together, catching knitted lip of cording in seams as close to cording as possible. Leave a 6-inch (15-cm) opening for turning.

7. Clip and press seams as needed. Turn and press. Slip-stitch opening closed.

8. Position cover in basket and tie cording around basket handles.

Old-Fashioned Embroidered Linens

*T*hree simple embroidery stitches and an assortment of pastel embroidery flosses are all you need to turn purchased pillowcases into luxurious linens reminiscent of the ones you might find in your grandmother's closet. They are easy to embroider and can be finished in an afternoon.

Embroidered Corner Design

- Purchased pillowcases
- Embroidery needle
- Embroidery floss: variegated pastel
- Dressmaker's pencil

1. Using a dressmaker's pencil, draw a triangle in one corner of a pillowcase, 1 inch (2.5 cm) from the edge of the closed end and the left seam. The two short sides of the triangle should measure approximately 5 inches (12.5 cm).

2. Using a lazy daisy stitch for flower petals (see page 9), randomly embroider flowers in various colors inside the triangle. Finish flowers by adding a French knot (see page 9) in the center of each.

3. To complete the design, randomly scatter French knots in various colors inside the triangle. Repeat process to make a matching pillowcase.

Honeymoon Travel Tips

• Assemble a "just-in-case" first-aid kit in a resealable plastic bag. Include aspirin, allergy medication, moist towelettes, alcohol pads, nail clippers, and adhesive strips.

• Pack half of your clothes and half of your husband's clothes in each suitcase. If one piece of luggage gets lost, then you both will still have something to wear. Along the same lines, each of you should have credit cards and money.

Embroidered Heart Design

Materials

- Purchased pillowcases
- Embroidery needle
- Embroidery floss: green, lavender, blue, yellow, pink, and white
- Dressmaker's pencil

Instructions

1. Referring to the instructions on page 10, transfer the heart design to the center of a pillowcase, 4 inches (10 cm) from the edge of the open end.

2. Using a dressmaker's pencil, lightly write the couple's name and wedding date in the center of the heart. Variations in letter size and the positioning of words will give the design an old-fashioned, hand-written look.

3. Once the entire pattern has been transferred to the pillowcase, embroider over the pattern. Use a backstitch for the flower stems and words (see page 8), a lazy daisy stitch for petals and leaves (see page 9), and a French knot for flower centers, flowers, and dots (see page 9). Repeat process to make a matching pillowcase.

Honeymoon Travel Tip

If you will be crossing several time zones, avoid caffeine and alcohol and drink plenty of water during the flight. Try to go to bed early several days before you leave and get as much sleep as possible on the flight. Once you arrive, switch your watch to local time as quickly as possible.

CREATIVE IDEAS FOR JOURNALS AND SCRAPBOOKS

appy memories make the best souvenirs, but it never hurts to take photographs, record your thoughts, and collect memorabilia that will remind you of that summer moonlit dance or a delightful lunch at a seaside restaurant. Here are some ideas to help you create a one-of-a-kind memory album.

• When saving memorabilia and recording your experiences, think beyond conventional scrapbooks and journals. The point is to make your memory book as interesting and descriptive as possible. Keep in mind that it's also important to record the small, ordinary items, such as what you had for your first dinner as newlyweds or a list of potential names you have picked out for a baby.

• When you're on a trip, pick up small items that can later be pasted into a scrapbook or journal. Matches, coasters, napkins, flyers, ticket stubs, and receipts are but a few of the freebies you can use to remember your travels. Also, consider saving items to record your first year of marriage. Sometimes, a grocery receipt can tell more about you at a particular point in your life than a picture can.

• If you save newspaper clippings, treat them with the following recipe to keep them from yellowing. Pour one capful of Milk of Magnesia into a bottle of club soda. Replace the cap and slowly turn the bottle upside down to mix. Store overnight in the refrigerator. The next day, pour the solution into a glass bowl or baking dish. Place the newspaper clipping in the solution for two minutes, then lay the clipping between white paper towels and carefully dab off the solution. Lift the clipping and place between two pages of thick white paper.

Weight the paper down with several books and leave overnight. Use only for newspaper prints; this process will make original ink bleed.

• Instead of purchasing background papers for your scrapbook, use maps, menus, train schedules, posters, and photocopies of favorite photographs.

• Avoid magnetic "press-and-stick" photo albums. The plastic covers often emit gases that yellow the photographs, and the sticky backing can permanently bond with the picture's paper backing.

• Take both black-and-white and color photographs. Color photos last only around fifty years; black-and-white photos have a hundred-year life expectancy.

• Use acid-free paper and pens in your scrapbook. Supplies are available from most craft and photography stores.

• Take time to write down interesting tidbits underneath photos and always date your photos. If the photo shows you sitting in a restaurant, write down what you had for dinner, why you were there, and who you were with.

Honeymoon Travel Journal

This travel journal is small enough to slip inside your purse or backpack, and is ideal for recording vacation schedules and honeymoon memories. You can make the journal any size you want; just vary the size of the mounting board and drawing paper. For the cover, you can also use paper from a travel magazine or scraps of travel-themed wallpaper or fabric.

- 2 pieces mounting board, 10 by 14 inches (25.5 by 35.5 cm)
- 2 pieces map paper, 6 by 8 inches (15 by 20.5 cm)
- 2 pieces map paper, 4½ by 6½ inches (11.5 by 16.5 cm)
- Sheets of drawing paper for pages
- 15 inches (38 cm) grosgrain ribbon, 1¼ inches (3 cm) wide
- Craft knife
- Straightedge
- Hot-glue gun and glue sticks
- Industrial hole punch

1. Using a craft knife and a straightedge, cut the mounting board into two 5- by 7-inch (12.5- by 18-cm) pieces.

2. To make the back of the journal, lay one piece of map paper face down on a flat surface. Remove paper from mounting board, center mounting board over map paper, and press in place. Trim each corner of paper ⅛ inch (.3 cm) from the corners of the board.

3. Apply a thin layer of hot glue to the edges all around the back of the board, then fold paper to the back of board, taking care that each corner is covered with paper. Let dry thoroughly.

4. Apply a thin layer of hot glue to back of one 4½- by 6½-inch (11.5 by 16.5 cm) piece of paper, center paper over inside of back cover, and press paper in place over edges of cover. Let dry. Repeat steps 2 through 4 to make the front of the journal.

5. With the craft knife and a straightedge, score the inside of the front cover 1½ inch (4 cm) from one edge to create a fold to make opening the journal easier.

6. Mark two holes on the left of the cover's opening fold, 2 inches (5 cm) from the top and the bottom and ¾ inch (2 cm) from the left edge.

7. For journal pages, cut drawing paper into 4- by 6-inch (10- by 15-cm) pieces. Make as many pages as desired.

8. Place pages between the front and back covers, aligning the pages with both covers along the left edge of journal. Punch holes with an industrial hole punch (available at copy shops).

9. Thread ribbon through holes and tie into a bow at the front of the journal.

Honeymoon Travel Tip

Soft-sided luggage is easier to manage than traditional hard-sided luggage. Choose a bag made of waterproof nylon that is washable, lightweight, and durable. It should have adjustable shoulder straps and industrial-strength zippers that can be locked.

HONEYMOON AT HOME

No time to get away after your wedding? Instead of sulking, make the most of your first week as newlyweds by planning cozy miniature getaways and intimate evenings. Here are some ideas to get you started—adapt them to suit your own personal style.

• Planning is the most important step for pulling off a honeymoon at home that you'll remember for years to come. A few weeks before the wedding, sit down and make an itinerary for your honeymoon week—just as if you were going on a trip. If you'll be working during the week, cook and freeze meals ahead of time so you can pull them out at a moment's notice. Have your wardrobe for the week planned out and have work clothes cleaned, ironed, and picked up from the cleaners. Splurge and have a housekeeper come midweek. The key is doing as much of your everyday routine ahead of time so you will have more time to enjoy each other.

• Take pictures throughout the week to document your "honeymoon." Have your photograph taken as your husband carries you across the threshold of your home, take snapshots of each other opening wedding presents, or photograph your "firsts," such as the first time you sit down to dinner together as newlyweds.

• Before your first night at home together, give your bedroom a romantic "re-do." Scatter rose petals on the floor and the bed, place a vase of fresh flowers on the nightstand, purchase a variety of massage oils and lotions (or make your

own using the recipes on page 94), place several candles around the room, have champagne chilling in the refrigerator, and invest in lingerie and robes for you both.

• Plan a sunrise picnic for two. Pack fresh fruit, bagels, and champagne in a picnic basket and head for the nearest park. If you prefer someplace a little more private, spread a blanket on your living room floor and have a picnic inside.

• Instead of opening all of your wedding gifts the day after the wedding, save them and open several each night of the following week.

• Plan miniature getaways throughout the week to places in your town that the two of you haven't been. If you usually go to professional baseball games, get tickets for the local college team or a minor league team. Request a tour of the most romantic exhibits at a local museum. Pack a picnic lunch and a blanket and scout out nature trails in your area.

• Buy a book on massage. After a long, relaxing bath, practice techniques on each other.

• Plan a romantic evening at home. Order carryout from your favorite restaurant and dine by candlelight to songs from your courtship days; then settle back on the sofa and watch videos of classic love stories.

Honeymoon Peignoir

*P*retty lingerie doesn't have to cost a fortune. It's easy to jazz up purchased gowns and robes with bits of lace and ribbon; small pieces of expensive imported lace go a long way if used as elegant accents along borders and sleeves. For additional embellishment, add lace and ribbons around the bottom edge of peignoir or scatter ribbon rosettes or beads across the bodice.

Materials

- Purchased silk or satin gown with spaghetti straps
- Wedding lace with pearls
- Needle with matching thread

Instructions

1. To determine the length of wedding lace needed, lay the lace across the front and over both shoulders of the gown. Add 1 inch (2.5 cm) and cut lace to that measurement. If you want to use thicker lace on your peignoir, cut twice as much lace and stitch the two pieces of lace together lengthwise.

2. Pin lace to gown as desired along front and over shoulders of gown; stitch in place. Trim loose threads.

3. With needle and matching thread, turn raw edges of lace under at the back end of each strap and stitch in place.

Honeymoon Travel Set

These pretty, yet practical travel accessories are handy for travel, whether you're going on an extended honeymoon or just an overnight trip. The travel set includes a carry-all tote, a shoe bag, a jewelry roll, and padded hangers with sachets. For durability, stitch the totes from heavy fabric, such as cotton duck or corduroy, and use patterned accent fabric for lining. The set also makes a great wedding gift for a couple on the go.

Carry-All Tote

- 1½ yards (1.4 m) cotton duck fabric
- 1½ yards (1.4 m) cotton fabric (for lining)
- 3 yards (2.75 m) woven jute braid, ⅝ inch (1.6 cm) wide

Instructions

Note: All seams are ½ inch (1.5 cm).

1. From the duck fabric, cut two 15- by 17-inch (38- by 43-cm) pieces for the body of the carry-all, two 15- by 9-inch (38- by 23-cm) pieces for the pockets, one 5- by 47-inch (12.5- by 119.5-cm) piece for the outer edges of the carry-all, and two 4- by 49-inch (10- by 124.5-cm) pieces for the straps.

2. From the cotton fabric, cut two 15- by 15-inch (38- 38-cm) pieces and one 5- by 47-inch (12.5- by 119.5-cm) piece.

3. Begin with the two 4- by 49-inch (10- by 124.5-cm) strap pieces; fold the raw edges of the fabric to the center so that they overlap to make 2-inch-wide (5-cm) straps; press. Center braid over raw edges and topstitch along both sides of braid. Make sure all raw edges of duck fabric are covered.

4. To make the pockets, turn ¼ inch (.5 cm) under twice on one lengthwise edge of each pocket piece and topstitch. Position one pocket along bottom of each 15- by 17-inch (38- by 43-cm) bag piece. With raw edges aligned, baste pocket in place along sides and bottom edges.

5. For strap placement, lay each 15- by 17-inch (38- by 43-cm) bag piece flat, with right sides up. Position each strap 3 inches (7.5 cm) from the sides, aligning raw edges along the bottom of the bag. Stitch straps and pocket pieces to the bag from the bottom of the bag to the top of the pockets.

6. To make the sides and bottom of the bag, with right sides together and raw edges aligned, baste the 5- by 47-inch (12.5- by 119.5-cm) piece down one side of the bag, across the bottom, and back up other side. Stitch in place; press and clip seams as needed. Repeat for the other side of the bag. Repeat step 6 to make bag lining.

7. Turn top raw edge of bag under ½ inch (1.5 cm), then down 1½ inches (4 cm); press in place. With wrong sides together, position lining inside the bag. Pin top raw edge of lining under the hem of the bag. Adjust straps and pin in place along top edge of bag. Stitch over lining and through straps, ¼ inch (.5 cm) from the folded edge of the hem. Topstitch again ¼ inch (.5 cm) from the top edge of the bag, making sure to catch straps in seam.

Honeymoon Travel Tip

If you plan to do a lot of shopping, pack an empty tote bag inside your suitcase to carry your souvenirs home.

Jewelry Roll

- ½ yard (.45 m) cotton duck fabric
- ½ yard (.45 m) cotton fabric (for lining)
- ½ yard (.45 m) polyester batting
- ⅔ yard (.6 m) woven jute braid, ⅝ inch (1.6 cm) wide

Instructions

Note: All seams are ½ inch (1.5 cm).

1. For jewelry roll, cut a 17- by 10-inch (43- by 25.5-cm) piece from the duck fabric, lining fabric, and the batting. Cut two 12- by 9-inch (30.5- by 23-cm) pieces from the lining fabric for the pockets.

2. Layer the batting on the wrong side of the duck fabric and machine-quilt batting and duck fabric together in a pattern of your choice. (We used a ½-inch-square (1.5-cm) pattern here.)

3. Locate the center of the 17- by 10-inch (43- by 25.5-cm) quilted piece. Position center of 24-inch (61-cm) piece of braid at this center

Diagram 1

right side of fabric

stitching line

fabric for Pocket

wrong side of fabric

point on the right side of the fabric; stitch center of braid in place.

4. Fold pocket pieces in half with wrong sides of lining fabric together and press.

5. Lay out flat the remaining 17- by 10-inch (43- by 25.5-cm) piece of lining fabric. Unfold one pocket piece and align one raw edge of pocket, with right sides together, on the 7-inch (18-cm) mark on the lining (Diagram 1). Stitch pocket piece to the lining. Fold under remaining raw edge of pocket, and fold pocket piece up and pin in place, aligning sides of the lining and the pocket. See Diagram 2.

Diagram 2

stitching line

Fold fabric up, matching raw edges.

Diagram 3

folded fabric edge
Pocket

seam line

folded fabric edge

Pocket

6. With right sides together and raw edges aligned, position second folded pocket piece along the bottom edge of the lining piece. Pin or baste pocket to hold in place. See Diagram 3.

7. With right sides together and raw edges aligned, stack lining and

outside of jewelry roll together. (Be sure to tuck tie ends inside so as not to catch them in stitching.) Stitch the pieces together, leaving a 6-inch (15-cm) opening for turning. Press seams and turn, then press again. Slip-stitch opening closed.

8. Fold jewelry roll over and tie. Knot the ends of braid and fringe.

Shoe Bag *(see page 92)*

Materials

- ⅔ yard (.6 m) cotton duck fabric
- ⅔ yard (.6 m) cotton fabric (for lining)
- 1 yard (.9 m) woven jute braid, ⅝ inch (1.6 cm) wide

Instructions

Note: All seams are ½ inch (1.5 cm).

1. Cut one 21- by 17-inch (53.5- by 43-cm) piece from both the cotton duck and the lining fabric.

2. Fold cotton duck fabric lengthwise, with right sides together, and stitch edges together. Press seams open. Repeat step 2 with lining fabric.

3. With right sides together and top raw edges aligned, place the lining inside the cotton duck fabric and machine-stitch lining and bag together. Machine-stitch across bottom edge of duck fabric piece, then machine-stitch bottom

edge of lining piece, leaving a 6-inch (15-cm) opening for turning. Press seams and turn. Slip-stitch opening closed.

4. Turn lining to inside of bag; press and top-stitch ½ inch (1.5 cm) from the top of the bag.

5. Position the center of 1 yard (.9 m) of jute braid at the center of the back of the bag, 2 inches (5 cm) from the top edge; stitch center of braid in place. Pull braid around to the front of bag and tie. Tie knots at ends of the braid and fringe.

Padded Hangers

- Fabric scraps (possibly left over from travel set)
- 2 plastic clothes hangers
- Craft paper
- Batting

For Round Sachet

- Fabric scraps
- 1 teaspoon lavender seeds or a small sachet of your choice
- Fiberfill stuffing
- 18 inches (45.5 cm) ivory satin ribbon, $\frac{1}{8}$ inch (.3 cm) wide

For Square Sachet

- Cedar shavings, potpourri, or a sachet of your choice
- $6\frac{1}{2}$-inch (16.5-cm) square of duck fabric
- 12 inches (30.5 cm) braided jute, $\frac{5}{8}$ inch (1.6 cm) wide
- 1-inch-diameter (2.5-cm) button

Instructions

Note: All seams are $\frac{1}{2}$ inch (1.5 cm).

1. Position a plastic hanger on a piece of craft paper and draw around hanger. Measure out from the drawn line 1 inch (2.5 cm) on all sides.

2. Using the hanger pattern you've created on the craft paper, cut two pieces from the fabric.

From the batting, cut two 3-inch-wide (7.5-cm) pieces to the same width as the hanger.

3. Wind batting around hanger so hanger is padded at least $\frac{1}{2}$-inch (1.5-cm) thick on all sides.

4. With right sides together and raw edges aligned, stitch fabric pieces together along the top edges, leaving a 1-inch (2.5-cm) opening at the center top for the hanger's hook. Press seams open.

5. Position fabric over padded hanger, threading hanger hook through the hole in top opening. Beginning at the center bottom, turn raw edges of fabric under $\frac{1}{2}$ inch (1.5 cm) and pin in place. Work from the center to the outside of the hanger, adjusting fabric as needed. Slip-stitch bottom of hanger closed, then slip-stitch opening at the top around hanger hook.

6. To make a round sachet, place lavender seeds or potpourri and a golf ball-sized piece of fiberfill stuffing in the center of the circle. Fold fabric up around potpourri and fiberfill. Wrap ribbon around fabric twice and tie into a knot. Knot ends of ribbon to form loop for hanging.

7. To make a square sachet, fold a square of duck fabric in half and stitch along one side and bottom. Press seam and turn so that seam is to the inside. Fill with cedar shavings or potpourri. Fringe raw edge of bag. Fold pouch down. Referring to the photograph, position braid with button on folded pouch, and tack button and braid through all layers of fabric.

8. Sachets can be draped over hanger or tucked in a drawer.

The Sensuous Bath

*N*othing washes away stress and anxiety better than a soothing, sensuous bath. Whether you need to relax or simply want to spend a romantic evening together, you can easily mix up a batch of bath salts, oils, and flower infusions to create the perfect mood. Once you've decided what you want to make, don't be afraid to mix herbs and oils to create personalized scents.

Choosing Herbs and Plants

The fragrance of herbs and flowers evokes a variety of feelings. The following list will help you choose which herbs to use in your concoctions.

Almond	Moisturizes, soothes
Calendula	Soothes, softens, and heals skin
Eucalyptus	Fragrant; good for muscle aches
Lady's-mantle	Heals; slightly astringent; good for dry skin
Lavender	Stimulates; adds fragrance; healing qualities and a gentle cleanser for all skin types
Lemon balm	Soothing and astringent; cleanses gently; fragrant
Lovage	Deodorizes
Rose	Refining and hydrating; fragrant; slightly astringent
Rosemary	Stimulates; invigorates; good for oily skin; boosts circulation
Scented Geraniums	Adds fragrance
Valerian	Soothes nerves

Custom Concoctions

Aromatherapy Massage Oil. Pamper each other with a custom mix of aromatic massage oil. If you want to make the oil from fresh herbs or dried flowers, cut the herbs, place them in a jar, then fill jar with almond oil. Place the mixture in the sun for at least eight hours. Strain the herbs from the oil, then add new herbs to the jar. Repeat this process at least six times—the more you repeat it, the more fragrant the oil will become. If you use essential oils, add eight to ten drops of each essential oil to the almond oil. Keep in mind that almond oil will stay fresh for only two to three months.

Fragrant Sea Salts. Light a few candles, pour yourself a glass of wine, then slip into a warm, fragrant bath. It's a relaxing way to wind down a romantic evening. Bath salts soothe the skin and keep longer than bath oils. To make bath salts, mix 1 cup (320 g) of coarse sea salt with food

coloring, adding 3 drops at a time until the desired color is achieved. Add about 25 drops of essential oil in your favorite scent. Store in a jar, keeping the lid tightly closed so the oils won't evaporate. For each bath, add 6 tablespoons of bath salts to the bath water.

Rosebud Footbath. At the end of a long, stressful day, soak your feet in a luxurious rosebud footbath. Begin by filling a jar with dried rosebuds. Pour boiling water over the rosebuds until the jar is filled with liquid; let steep for 15 minutes. Strain the liquid into a footbath and add very warm water and 1 tablespoon of sea salts; stir to dissolve. Keep a bath towel nearby so that, after soaking your feet, you can easily pat them dry. If you want to make a double batch, pour the strained liquid into a bottle. This footbath will keep for about one week.

Soothing Epsom Salts. A variation on sea salts is to mix Epsom salts with borax and fragrance. Use 2 cups (640 g) of Epsom salts, 6 to 8 drops of food coloring, 2 tablespoons of borax, and 6 to 8 drops of essential oil. If you have trouble mixing the food coloring with the salts, mix it first with the borax, then add the salts slowly.

Beeswax and Aloe Vera Hand Lotion. After you've soaked in a relaxing bath, pamper your skin with the natural moisturizers of beeswax and aloe vera gel. Place a 4-ounce (113 g) bottle of vegetable glycerin and a chunk of beeswax (about the size of two ice cubes) into a glass dish and microwave at 30-second intervals until the beeswax melts. Add 1 cup (245 g) of aloe vera gel, 1 teaspoon of vitamin E oil, and 4 to 6 drops of almond extract; mix carefully in a food processor until the mixture is well blended. Pour the mixture into a jar while it is still warm.

Silky Body Powders. Baby your body with a custom blend of body powder. Combine 2 cups (250 g) cornstarch with ¼ cup (63 g) baking soda. Add several drops of your favorite essential oil and mix well.

Oatmeal Bath. Mix 1 cup (81 g) oatmeal with ½ cup (160 g) sea salt, ¼ cup (30 g) powdered milk, and ¼ cup (7 g) dried lavender or other dried herbs. Pour the mixture into a muslin tea bag and place over the faucet when drawing a bath.

Pretty Packaging

Give your personalized bath products a professional look by creating labels and adornments for the jars and bottles.

- Purchase labels from an office supply store and print out the name of each product on the label, either on a computer or by hand. If desired, embellish the labels with paints, rubber stamps, embossers, or markers.

- Use ribbons, thin wire, and leftovers of dried herbs and flowers to make small wreaths and decorations for the bottles and jars.

- Store your bath products in recycled salad dressing bottles, small jelly jars, silver shakers, and decorative boxes.

- Apply sealing wax or shrink-wrap sealers around the tops of bottles and jars.

Elegant Wine Pouches

$\mathcal{S}$end off the happy couple with a bottle of wine packaged in one of these attractive, easy-to-make fabric pouches. We've used two different fabrics, double-sided satin and loosely woven hemp cloth; either fabric creates a soft, attractive container. Although these bags are handy in helping prevent wine bottles from breaking, they can be also reused as gift bags.

Satin Wine Bag

- Double-sided satin fabric, amount will vary
- 1 yard (.9 m) ivory tulle with pearl trim
- 1 large sheer white fabric rose (with wire)
- 2 small sheer white fabric roses

Instructions

Note: All seams on wine pouches are ½ inch (1.5 cm).

1. Measure wine bottle and add 3 inches (7.5 cm) to the width and height, then cut a piece of satin fabric to this measurement.

2. With right sides together and raw edges aligned, fold fabric in half and stitch along long seam. Referring to the instructions on page 10, finish seam with a mock flat-fell seam.

3. Stitch along bottom edge of fabric. Press and turn bag.

4. Turn raw edges under ½ inch (1.5 cm) twice along the top edge of the bag and stitch. Place wine bottle inside bag, wrap tulle with pearl trim around the neck of the bottle twice and loosely tie trim into a square knot. Trim ends of tulle and pearl trim.

5. Tack small fabric roses approximately 1½ inch (4 cm) from the ends of the tulle. Wrap wire of large fabric rose around knotted tulle and trim.

Hemp Bag

- Loosely woven hemp fabric, amount will vary
- 24 inches (61 cm) flat jute braid, ½ inch (1.5 cm) wide
- Stems of lavender, approximately seven

Instructions

1. Measure wine bottle and add 3 inches (7.5 cm) to the width and height, then cut a piece of hemp fabric to this measurement.

2. With right sides together and raw edges aligned, fold fabric in half and stitch along long seam. Referring to instructions on page 10, finish seam with a mock flat-fell seam.

3. Stitch along bottom edge of fabric. Press and turn bag.

4. Referring to the instructions on page 10, fringe 4 inches (10 cm) along the top edge of the bag. Measure and knot fringe at ½-inch (1.5-cm) intervals.

5. Place bag around wine bottle and tie the jute braid into a square knot, knot ends of braid, and trim. Slide lavender stems through knot. Tighten knot, if necessary.

Happily Ever After

*A*ppily ever after begins on your wedding day. As newlyweds, it is natural to experience growing pains as you create a new life together. No doubt you'll hear plenty of advice from family and friends. Our suggestion? Try to make each day as special as the first.

With this in mind, this chapter showcases an assortment of treasures and tips designed especially for celebrating a lifetime of love. Several projects of keepsake quality are featured here, from a collage tray assembled to commemorate your wedding to a cross-stitched sampler that is destined to become a family heirloom.

"Grow old along with me! The best is yet to be.
The last of life, for which the first was made. . ."

– Robert Browning

Heirloom Throw

Cuddle up on a chilly winter afternoon underneath this romantic throw. Purchased ribbon embroidery rosettes allow you to make the design in a fraction of the time you would spend making handmade rosettes—without sacrificing the heirloom quality of the throw.

– Afghan or loosely woven throw

– Assortment of ribbon embroidery appliqués

– 10 yards (9.2 m) pink ribbon, ⅛ inch (.3 cm) wide

– Tapestry needle, size 18 to 22

1. Using the pattern on this page as a guide, arrange an assortment of appliqués in a heart shape in one corner of the afghan. When you are satisfied with the arrangement, tack appliqués in place with a needle and coordinating thread.

2. If desired, center appliqués in every other block of the afghan and tack with needle and thread.

3. Using a tapestry needle, weave narrow pink ribbon down the center of each border. (Here, the ribbon has been woven every two stitches.)

4. Referring to the instructions on page 10, fringe the edges of the afghan or throw. (It may already have fringed edges.)

Honeymoon Tip

You never know when you might need a sewing kit with a needle, thread, safety pins, and buttons. Adhesive tape is available that can be ironed onto clothing to hem clothes in a snap.

Golden Candlesticks and Candles

*D*ress up plain crystal candlesticks with gold paint, wire, and gold beads. For an even more sophisticated look, use gold-studded candles with the candlesticks. If you light the candles at the wedding, blow them out before they burn to the ends, then use them again on your first anniversary.

Materials

- Crystal candlesticks
- Acrylic paint, antique gold
- Glaze sealer
- 22-gauge wire
- Small gold beads
- Paintbrush
- Small needle-nose pliers
- Pencil
- White candles
- Miniature hot-glue gun

Instructions

1. Use the gold acrylic paint to create highlights on the crystal candlesticks. The candlesticks we chose have cut grooves along the bottom. To highlight the grooves, brush gold paint over the grooved area. Wipe off any excess paint. Paint should seep into grooves of design—with bits of glass showing through. When the paint is completely dry, brush candlesticks with glaze to seal.

2. Cut wire into two 12-inch (30.5-cm) lengths (one for each candle). Use needle-nose pliers to make a tiny loop at one end of the wire.

3. Thread one bead on the wire, then begin coiling wire around a pencil, adding a bead every one to two coils.

4. Finish the end of the wire with a tiny loop.

5. Remove coiled wire from pencil. Stretch coil out to fit around candlestick. Loop ends of wire together and adjust wire as needed. (You may want to make several coils for each candlestick.)

6. To embellish candles, use a miniature hot-glue gun without the glue stick. Carefully melt a tiny indention in the candle and insert bead quickly before wax cools. Place beads around candles in a pleasing manner.

Lace Collage Tray

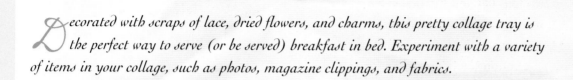

Decorated with scraps of lace, dried flowers, and charms, this pretty collage tray is the perfect way to serve (or be served) breakfast in bed. Experiment with a variety of items in your collage, such as photos, magazine clippings, and fabrics.

Materials

- Wooden frame, 11 x 14 inches (28 x 35.5 cm)
- Gold metallic acrylic paint
- Crackle medium for acrylic painting
- Ivory acrylic paint
- 2 burnished brass cabinet door handles (with screws)
- White rice paper, 11 x 14 inches (28 x 35.5 cm)
- Scraps of bridal laces, trims, motifs, and ribbons
- Dried white rose petals
- Sprigs of dried baby's breath
- Brass charms
- Fine-grade sandpaper (optional)
- Wallpaper, contact paper, or felt backing (optional)
- Paintbrush
- Fabric glue
- Clothespins

Instruction

1. Remove glass and backing from the frame. If necessary, sand frame before painting. Paint frame with gold paint; allow to dry. Following manufacturer's directions, apply crackle medium over gold paint. Use ivory paint for the final coat. Allow to dry thoroughly.

2. Position one handle at the center of each side of the frame and attach with screws.

3. Lay cardboard backing right side up and cover with rice paper. Add spots of fabric glue in corners to secure paper. Arrange laces, ribbons, and trims as desired; secure pieces with fabric glue. Scatter dried rose petals, sprigs of baby's breath, and charms over arrangement; secure pieces with fabric glue.

4. Trim excess materials along the edges of the cardboard backing. Place glass on top. (Use clothespins to hold glass and backing together as you turn the arrangement over to place in the frame.) Position glass and backing in frame. If desired, back of tray can be finished by applying a backing, such as wallpaper, contact paper, or felt.

Monogrammed Pillow

The quilted organdy square on this monogrammed pillow contrasts nicely with a background of beautiful brocade cotton. In the center, braided cording creates an interesting raised monogram. You could also monogram the pillow with stitching on your sewing machine, but the cording requires less time and precision and provides an interesting texture.

- 6½-inch (16.5-cm) square of white organdy fabric
- 6½-inch (16.5-cm) square of batting
- Two 12-inch (30.5-cm) squares of ivory brocade cotton fabric
- ¾ yard (.7 m) ivory flat braid, ½ inch (1.5 cm) wide
- 18 inches (45.5 cm) ivory silk cording, ¼ inch (.5 cm) wide (amount will vary, depending on chosen letter)
- 1½ yards (1.4 m) ivory flat fringe braid, 1 inch (2.5 cm) wide
- 12-inch (30.5 cm) pillow form

Instructions

Note: All seams are ½ inch (1.5 cm).

1. Position organdy fabric over batting and quilt in ½-inch (1.5 cm) squares.

2. Referring to the photograph, place quilted square, right side up, diagonally on one 12-inch (30.5-cm) square of brocade; hand-stitch in place.

3. Stitch ½-inch (1.5-cm) flat braid around organdy to frame.

4. Find center of quilted piece. Arrange cording on quilted piece to form the desired letter. (Some letters, such as B, E, and F, may require cutting the cording into several pieces.) Experiment with a piece of yarn or string until you get the look you want.

5. When you are pleased with the monogram letter, pin cording in place and hand-stitch cording to quilted piece, using coordinating thread.

6. Measure ¾ inch (2 cm) from the edge of the pillow top. Place the 1-inch (2.5-cm) fringe braid along this line. Position fringe braid with the fringe point out around pillow top, adjusting for corners as needed. Stitch braid to pillow top.

7. With right sides together and raw edges aligned, stack pillow top and pillow bottom together and stitch pieces together, leaving a 6-inch (15-cm) opening for turning. (To prevent catching the fringe in seam when stitching, pin edge away from seam.) Press seams open and turn. Insert pillow form and slip-stitch opening closed.

Caring for Fine Linens

• To remove stubborn spots from stained linens, add equal parts of a detergent designed for mild cleansing and a nonchlorine color-safe bleach into a washing machine full of hot water. Soak linens for at least three hours, then wash and rinse with hot water. Repeat process until stains disappear.

• Yellowed fabrics can be lightened by soaking in extremely diluted nonchlorine bleach; try ½ cup (120 ml) of dry oxygen bleach to 3 gallons (11.5 l) of water. Soak until the fabric is white.

• When ironing linens, spray them frequently with water to keep them damp. Avoid using starch.

Picnic Blanket

he corner pockets on this great picnic blanket create storage for flatware and matching napkins. When the blanket is folded up, it fits easily inside a picnic basket or backpack.

- 2 yards (1.8 m) ticking, 60 inches (152 cm) wide
- 2 yards (1.8 m) red-checked cotton fabric
- 9 yards (8.3 m) purchased bias stripping (optional)

1. Cut a 60-inch (152-cm) square from the ticking for the blanket. From the remaining ticking, cut four 11-inch (28-cm) squares for the pockets.

2. From the red-checked fabric, cut four 18-inch (45.5-cm) squares for the napkins. Use the remaining checked fabric to cut 1½-inch (4-cm) bias strips (see page 11). Piece strips together to create strips that total 9 yards (8.3 m) in length. (Purchased bias tape can also be used. You will need 9 yards [8.3 m] double-fold strips, 1 inch [2.5 cm] wide.)

3. To make pockets, fold one 11-inch (28-cm) square diagonally with wrong sides together and raw edges aligned. (The pockets will be double thickness.) Press along the fold line.

4. With right sides together and raw edges aligned, stitch bias strip along diagonal edge of pocket. Fold bias strip over, press, and topstitch in place. Repeat step 4 for the three remaining pockets.

5. To attach pockets, pin pockets to each corner of the square of ticking. Stitch pockets in place along the edge of blanket.

6. To make napkin slot, measure and mark 5 inches (12.5 cm) from either side of top edge of the pocket. Topstitch a line at a 90° angle from the pocket top to the blanket's edge. Repeat step 6 for the three remaining pockets.

7. Once pockets are attached, stitch bias strip along the edges of the blanket with right sides together and raw edges aligned. Fold bias strip over edge and topstitch in place.

8. Finish napkin squares by turning raw edges under twice to make a ¼-inch (.5-cm) hem and topstitch. Fold napkins and place one napkin in the slot of each pocket.

Easy Picture Frames

*P*riceless wedding photographs shouldn't be stored in just any frame. A variety of purchased frames are easily transformed into charming, one-of-a-kind photograph displays. Regardless of the style you choose, you'll find all of these decorative frames simple and easy to make.

Whitewashed Twigs. This twig frame proves that natural materials never go out of style. All you need is a wooden frame at least 2 inches (5 cm) wide on each side and some straight twigs about ⅛ inch (.3 cm) in diameter. Using garden shears, cut the twigs to the length of the sides of the frame, then glue twig pieces in place around the frame using a hot-glue gun and glue sticks, placing the twigs as close together as possible. Alternating the direction of the twigs in a pattern creates a nice texture. When the glue is completely dry, whitewash the twigs with a light coat of white paint.

All Wrapped Up. Use scraps of gift wrap to decorate a frame. Begin by covering a frame with a solid or printed gift wrap (we used white-on-white wrap for this frame), securing paper with craft glue. Cut individual designs from decorative gift wrap, arrange designs as desired on top of the frame, and secure with craft glue. Seal the paper design with several coats of clear acrylic sealer. When the sealer is dry, apply crackle medium according to manufacturer's instructions. Finish the frame by lightly painting it with a dark brown glaze.

Surrounded by Seashells. The shells you picked up on a romantic walk on the beach can be put to good use decorating a frame. Beginning with the larger shells, hot-glue shells to a wooden frame, then use smaller shells to fill in the gaps. Continue gluing shells onto the frame until the entire frame is covered.

Topped with a Bow. This frame is as simple as it looks. All you do is find a frame in the desired color (if you can't find one, paint your own), then hot-glue a bow to the top of the frame.

Lavender and Lace. Use leftover lace from your wedding gown to cover a frame. Stretch the lace tautly across the front and sides of the frame and glue in place. Fold the ends of the lace to the back side and glue. When glue is dry, carefully trim the lace along the inside edges of the frame. Glue a border of cording along the inside edge of the frame opening, beginning and ending in the lower right corner. (If desired, glue a silk rosette over the ends of the cord.) Position stems of lavender and baby's breath at the top center of the frame and glue in place. Thread a piece of ⅛-inch-wide (.3-cm) ribbon through a button, then tie ribbon into a bow. Glue the button over the center of the lavender stems.

113

Glass Act. Add style to a floating glass frame with pressed flowers and foliage. Arrange the flowers around the edge of the frame, position the photo in the center of the frame, then cover with the top piece of glass, and frame. If desired, you can trim the person from the photo for an interesting subject. A touch of clear-drying white craft glue will hold flowers in place.

Gilded Geometrics. Turn a flat frame into a three-dimensional accessory by gluing wooden triangles around the sides. Once the triangles are positioned as desired and glued in place, paint the frame and triangles white. When dry, crackle the frame following manufacturer's instructions. Let dry thoroughly, then lightly brush entire frame with gold paint.

Rosebud Frame. Dried rosebuds and a hot-glue gun are all you need to make this lovely floral frame (Rosebuds can be purchased by the ounce at your local grocery or health food market and some craft stores.) Beginning along the inside edge of the frame, attach rosebuds to a purchased frame with hot-glue gun. Continue around the frame, working to the outside edges. Finish off the sides of the frame by gluing decorative flat braid around the edge.

GIFT IDEAS FOR ANNIVERSARIES

An anniversary is an important milestone in a relationship. Though tradition dictates that you present each other with anniversary gifts, they don't have to be expensive to be rich with meaning. Sometimes the simplest gestures mean the most.

If you do decide to mark the occasion by splurging, choose something as a couple that will bring you years of memories or pleasure, such as a trip, a piece of fine furniture, or even china or crystal to finish your set.

Though it is unknown where the list of traditional and contemporary gifts originated, we believe they were probably created by retailers hoping to make money off the occasion. We've also listed some less-traditional, more creative gift ideas.

Year	Traditional Gifts	Ideas
1	Paper	Tickets to sporting events/concerts, gift certificates, books, handwritten poems, stocks
2	Cotton	Cozy blanket or bed linens (see page 80), clothing, quilt, embroidered handkerchief or bookmark
3	Leather	Journal, belt, handbag, leather picture frame, puppy with a leather collar
4	Fruit, flowers	Scented candles, linen with flower motifs, garden equipment, flower seeds, gourmet food items, scented bath products (see page 94), artwork with fruit or flower motifs
5	Wood	Hope chest (see page 30), jewelry box (see page 32), antique furniture, wooden figurines, garden trellis

Year	Traditional Gifts	Ideas
6	Candy, iron	Chocolates, wrought-iron furniture, candlesticks, gift certificate to a steak house (beef is high in iron!), wrought-iron gate, andirons for your fireplace
7	Copper, wool	Jewelry, decorative pots, clothing, blanket, a jar of pennies
8	Bronze, pottery	Dishes, candlesticks, statuary for the garden
9	Pottery, willow	Pottery classes, willow patio furniture, Christmas ornaments (see page 56), picnic basket, weeping willow seedling
10	Tin, aluminum	Gifts wrapped in foil or tucked into a tin, imported boxes, money, tins of exotic teas

Year	Contemporary Gifts	Ideas
1	Clocks	Watch, grandfather clock, desk clock with engraved plaque that says "Our love is timeless," cuckoo clock, small hourglass, sundial
2	China	Pieces to match your china, candlesticks (see page 104), a trip to China, figurines, miniature china tea set
3	Crystal, glass	Vase, pieces to match your crystal, sunglasses, bookcase with glass doors, hand mirrors
4	Electric appliances	Stereo equipment, power tools, bread maker, mixer, indoor grill
5	Silverware	Pieces of silver, chimes, jewelry made of old silverware, knives, tea service
6	Wood	Hope chest (see page 30), jewelry box (see page 32), an antique piece of furniture, wooden figurines, a new deck
7	Desk sets	Handmade sets decoupaged with photos or covered with hand-made paper, engraved letter opener, desk lamp
8	Linens	Hand-embroidered pillowcases (see page 80), fine cotton sheets, monogrammed towels
9	Leather	Journal, belt, handbag, picture frame, puppy with a leather collar
10	Diamond Jewelry	Ring, necklace, a diamond in the rough

Remaining Years	Traditional	Contemporary
11	Steel	Fashion jewelry
12	Silk, linen	Pearls
13	Lace	Textiles, furs
14	Ivory	Gold jewelry
15	Crystal	Watches
20	China	Platinum
25	Silver	Silver
30	Pearls	Diamond
35	Coral	Jade
40	Rubies	Rubies
45	Sapphires	Sapphires
50	Gold	Gold
55	Emeralds	Emeralds
60	Diamond	Diamond
75	Diamond	Diamond

Redwork Christmas Tree Skirt and Stocking

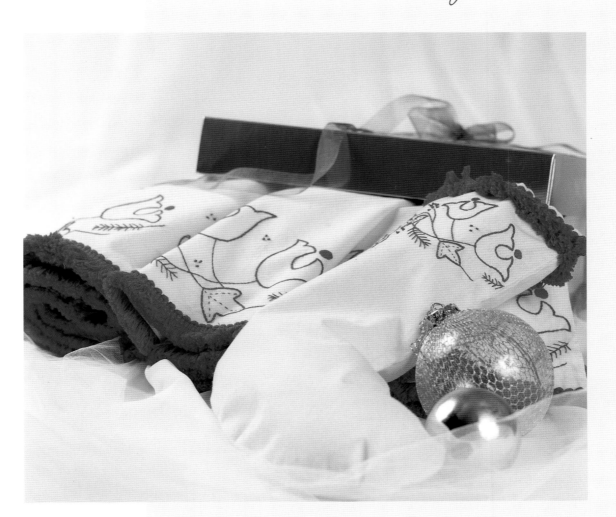

Start your own family traditions by stitching this old-fashioned tree skirt and stocking set. The striking design is a classic embroidery technique known as redwork, because all stitching is done with red embroidery floss. (If you prefer, you may use another color.) Though these projects are time-consuming (because of the amount of embroidery involved), the stitches themselves are basic and easy to execute. If you can't bear the thought of undertaking so much stitching, trace the pattern with dimensional fabric paint.

Note: All seams are ½ inch (1.5 cm). To set color of floss, soak skeins in solution of 1 tablespoon white vinegar and 1 cup (240 ml) cold water; rinse floss thoroughly and let dry.

Tree Skirt

- 8 yards muslin, 45 inches (114.5 cm) wide
- 1¼ yards (1.15 m) string
- Pattern on page 119
- Tracing paper
- 12 skeins red embroidery floss
- Embroidery needle, size 9 or 10
- 6¼ yards (5.75 m) red cotton fringe, 1 inch (2.5 cm) wide
- 2 hooks and eyes
- Pushpin
- Dressmaker's pencil
- Iron

1. Cut muslin into four 2-yard (1.85 m) pieces. With selvages aligned, stitch two pieces of the muslin together lengthwise along one edge. Repeat step 1 with remaining two muslin pieces.

2. Referring to the cutting diagram, fold one muslin piece in half and then into fourths. To make outer circle, tie pushpin to one end of string. Stick pushpin through folded corner of muslin. Measure 36 inches (91.5 cm) of the string and tie loose end of the string to a dressmaker's pencil to make a compass. Holding string taut, draw an arc with a 36-inch (91.5-cm) radius on muslin.

3. To mark inner circle, draw an arc with a 1½-inch (4-cm) radius in same manner (see step 2). Cut through all layers. Open skirt; cut a straight line from the outer edge to the inner circle to create an opening. Repeat for the remaining muslin piece.

4. Enlarge pattern on page 119 to 185%. Referring to the instructions on page 10, transfer the embroidery design 2 inches (5 cm) from the outer edge of one muslin circle, repeating the pattern approximately 16 times around muslin. Embroider design using two strands of floss. (Refer to page 8 for embroidery stitches.)

5. With right sides together and raw edges aligned, stitch muslin pieces together, leaving an 8-inch (20.5-cm) opening along the straight edge of the skirt opening. Clip curves and turn. Slip-stitch opening closed. Press.

6. Topstitch fringe to outer edge of skirt. Stitch one hook and one eye 2 inches (5 cm) from the inner circle on the wrong side of the skirt opening. Stitch remaining hook and eye 7 inches (18 cm) from the inner circle.

Stocking

- Pattern (on this page)
- Tracing paper
- ½ yard (.5 m) muslin, 45 inches (114.5 cm) wide
- 1 skein red embroidery floss
- Embroidery needle, size 9 or 10
- ½ yard (.5 m) red cotton fringe, 1 inch (2.5 cm) wide
- Dressmaker's pencil
- Iron

Instructions

1. Enlarge pattern to 125%. Referring to the instructions on page 10, transfer the stocking pattern to the muslin and cut out four pieces

2. Transfer the embroidery pattern (see page 10) 2 inches (5 cm) from the top edge of one stocking front. Embroider design, using two strands of floss. (Refer to page 8 for embroidery stitches.)

3. With right sides together and raw edges aligned, stitch embroidered stocking front to stocking back, leaving top open. Clip curves and turn. Press stocking flat.

4. To make the hanger, cut a 2- by 4-inch (5- x 10-cm) piece of muslin. Turn long edges under ½ inch (1.5 cm), then fold muslin in half lengthwise and topstitch both edges. Fold strip in half to make a loop. With right sides together, raw edges aligned, and the loop toward the center, baste the hanger to the top edge of the stocking back near left side seam.

5. To make lining, stitch together the remaining two muslin pieces, leaving the top edge open and a 3-inch (7.5-m) opening in the side seam above the heel. Clip curves but do not turn.

6. With right sides together, slip lining over stocking, matching side seams and top edges. Stitch lining to stocking around top edge, catching ends of hanger in seam. Turn stocking through opening in lining. Slip-stitch opening above heel closed. Tuck lining inside stocking.

7. Topstitch the fringe around top of stocking.

Wedding Sampler

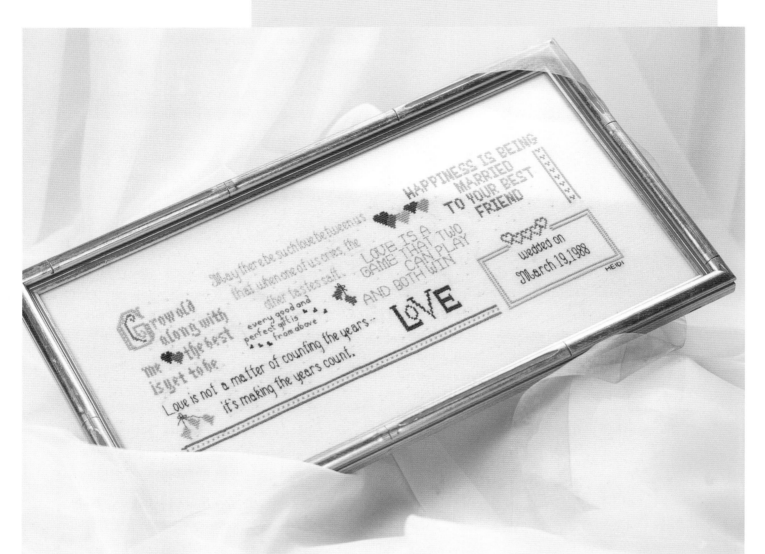

Happiness is being married to your best friend

May there be such love between us that when one of us cries, the other tastes salt.

Love is a game that two can play and both win

Grow old along with me the best is yet to be

every good and perfect gift is from above

Love

Love is not a matter of counting the years... it's making the years count.

wedded on March 19, 1988

HEIDI

The old-fashioned technique of cross-stitch gives this lovely wedding sampler its heirloom appeal. To personalize the sampler, add the wedding date and use embroidery floss that matches the color scheme of the wedding. You can also add your own favorite verses; create a pattern by writing the letters on cross-stitch graph paper.

— 18-count Aida cloth, even-weave muslin, or cross-stitch fabric, 24 x 14 inches (61 x 35.5 cm)

— Embroidery floss in five coordinating colors, plus silver floss for the background

— Embroidery needle

1. Referring to the pattern provided (see page 122), choose a floss color for each color on the pattern. You can use floss in the colors shown or choose a color scheme to coordinate with the wedding colors or the couple's home decor.

2. With a needle and two strands of floss, cross-stitch the design on the fabric, using the pattern provided as a guide. If using even-weave cloth, cross-stitch over two threads in the fabric.

3. When the cross-stitch design is finished, secure the thread ends and have the sampler professionally framed.

Sentimental Memories

*Y*ou'll be surprised at how the small special touches you make today will live on through tomorrow's cherished recollections of your wedding day. After all, happy memories make the best souvenirs.

• Keeping a journal is an excellent way to keep track of wedding plans. If you have never had luck keeping a journal, try instead to record day-to-day appointments and activities on a small calendar. Include dress fittings, meetings with the photographer and florist, and special days, such as your bridesmaids' luncheon. After the wedding, you'll be amazed at how soon you forget the hard work that goes into planning a wedding.

• A handmade ring bearer's pillow (see page 70) is sure to become a coveted heirloom. For an extra-special touch, pass along the pillow to sisters and friends for their wedding; then embroider each couple's name and wedding date inconspicuously on the bottom of the pillow.

• Be sure to have a guest book at all parties and at the wedding to record the names of friends and loved ones who attend.

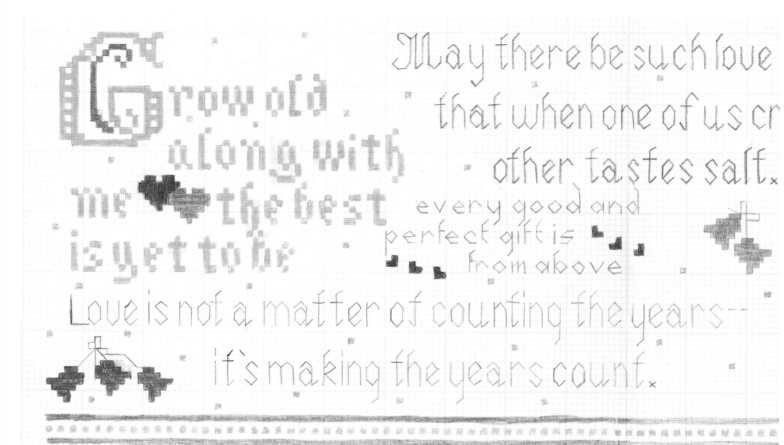

Grow old along with me ♥ the best is yet to be

May there be such love that when one of us cr other tastes salt.

every good and perfect gift is from above

Love is not a matter of counting the years-- it's making the years count.

Sentimental Memories

• For posterity's sake, explore your ideas on paper. Sketch your wedding dress, make lists of foods you would like to serve at the reception, and even attach fabric swatches and magazine cutouts. These will fit nicely into a pocket folder in your wedding album.

• Don't scrimp on wedding photography and videography. Although this may seem to be the easiest place to trim the budget, pho-tographs and videos will be all you have left once the big day has passed.

• Choose a wedding book with a three-ring binder such as the one on page 14. This allows you to add pages and pockets as needed for storing photographs and ideas.

• Take time to create a memory box (see page 16) for your keepsakes. You will be more

apt to save trinkets and tokens if you have a special place to store them.

- Have a "signature tablecloth" at each shower for guests to sign. When you have collected the signatures, embroider each name to create a reminder of happy times.

- If you have your wedding dress or brides-maids' dresses made by a seamstress, save scraps of fabric, lace, and trim. These bits and pieces can embellish a handmade garter that you make for a friend for her wedding day.

- After the wedding and honeymoon, choose your favorite photos and create a web site that friends and family can access. Add captions describing where you were, what you were doing, or what you were feeling at the time.

Supplier List and Acknowledgments

The authors would like to acknowledge the following companies for donating products used in many of these projects. Please check your local craft, hobby, or sewing center for materials. If you are unable to find what you need locally, you may contact these companies for information on where to find crafting supplies.

Artistic Wire Ltd.
PO Box 9663
Downers Grove, IL 60515
630-530-7567
Wire

B & B Etching Products, Inc.
18700 N. 107th Avenue, #13
Sun City, AZ 85373
602-815-9095
Etching supplies

Back Street, Inc.
3905 Steve Reynolds Blvd.
Norcross, GA 30093
770-381-7373
www.backstreetcrafts.com
Crackle medium

Bucilla Corporation
1 Oak Ridge Road
Hazleton, PA 18201
717-384-2525
www.bucilla.com
Silk ribbon for embroidery

C. M. Offray & Son, Inc.
360 Rt. 24
Chester, NJ 07930
908-879-4700
www.offray.com
Ribbon and trims

Charles Craft, Inc.
PO Box 1049
Laurinburg, NC 28353
910-844-3521
www:stitching.com/charlescraft
Cross stitch/embroidery supplies

Coats & Clark, Inc.
30 Patewood Drive, Ste #351
Greenville, SC 29615
864-281-5521
www.coatsandclark.com
Sewing and embroidery threads

Creative Beginnings
475 Morro Bay Boulevard
Morro Bay, CA 93442
805-772-9030
Brass and silver charms

Daler-Rowney USA
2 Corporate Drive
Cranbury, NJ 08512
609-655-5252
www.daler-rownery.com
Paper and art supplies

Delta Technical Coatings
2550 Pellissier Place
Whittier, CA 90601
213-686-0678
Acrylic paints

The DMC Corporation
10 Port Kearny
S. Kearny, NJ 07032
201-589-0606
www.dmc-usa.com
Embroidery threads

The Dow Chemical Co.
Customer Information Center
PO Box 1206
Midland, MI 48674
1-800-441-4369
Polystyrene

Duncan Enterprises
5673 E. Shields Avenue
Fresno, CA 93727
209-291-4444
www.duncan-enterprises.com
Acrylic paints

Foster, Inc.
PO Box 657
Wilton, ME 04294
207-645-2574
Wood pieces

Morning Glory Products
302 Highland Drive
Taylor, TX 76574
800-234-9105
Batting and stuffing

Nature's Pressed
PO Box 212
Orem, UT 84097
801-225-1169
Pressed flowers and foliage

NOVTEX Corp.
510 State Road
N. Adams, MA 01247
413-664-4509
Laces and trims

Peking Handicraft, Inc.
1388 San Mateo Avenue
San Francisco, CA 94080
415-871-3788
Crocheted doilies

Plaid Enterprises
1649 International Court
Norcross, GA 30093
770-923-8200
www.plaidonline.com
Acrylic paints and sealers

Regenboog Dried Flowers
1861 West Oak Parkway
Marietta, GA 30062
770-424-2867
www.regenboog.com
Dried flowers and foliage

Walnut Hollow
1409 State Road 23
Dodgeville, WI 53533-2112
608-935-2341
www.walnuthollow.com
Wood products

Westwater Enterprises LP
917 Mountain Avenue
Mountainside, NJ 07092
908-654-8871
Ribbon embroidery appliqués

Zweigart-Joan Toggitt, Ltd
2 Riverview Drive
Somerset, NJ 08873
732-271-1949
www.zweigart.com
Needlework supplies

In addition, many thanks to Andrea and Jamie Munn, the models for the chapter openers. For graciously assisting us with location photography, thanks to Tracy Munn (Asheville, NC), as well as the folks at Gourmet Gardens (Weaverville, NC) and Payne's Chapel (Sandy Mush, NC). Thank you to Hedy Fischer for allowing us the use of her car. And a very special thanks to Lamar Clemmons.